2nd Printing
Over 22,500 in Print

How To Be A Man of Character in A World of Compromise:
Devotional Insights From the Book of Proverbs
ISBN 1-56292-100-2

P.O. Box 54744
Tulsa, Oklahoma 74155

Published by Honor Books
P.O. Box 55388
Tulsa, Oklahoma 74155

How To Be a Man of Character in a World of Compromise

DEVOTIONAL INSIGHTS FROM THE BOOKS OF PROVERBS

by
Richard Exley

HB HONOR BOOKS

Tulsa, Oklahoma

Christmas 2000

Sweet Rob

DEDICATION

To Owen Carr,
a man whose life and ministry
exemplify the character
and integrity
taught in Proverbs.

Love & Prayers
Sharon &
Tony

Contents

PROVERBS 1

1 *The proverbs of Solomon son of David, king of Israel:*

2 *for attaining wisdom and discipline; for understanding words of insight;*

3 *for acquiring a disciplined and prudent life, doing what is right and just and fair;*

4 *for giving prudence to the simple, knowledge and discretion to the young—*

5 *let the wise listen and add to their learning, and let the discerning get guidance—*

6 *for understanding proverbs and parables, the sayings and riddles of the wise.*

7 *The fear of the* LORD *is the beginning of knowledge, but fools despise wisdom and discipline.*

8 *Listen, my son, to your father's instruction and do not forsake your mother's teaching.*

9 *They will be a garland to grace your head and a chain to adorn your neck.*

10 *My son, if sinners entice you, do not give in to them.*

11 *If they say, "Come along with us; let's lie in wait for someone's blood, let's waylay some harmless soul;*

12 *let's swallow them alive, like the grave, and whole, like those who go down to the pit;*

13 *we will get all sorts of valuable things and fill our houses with plunder;*

14 *throw in your lot with us, and we will share a common purse"—*

15 *my son, do not go along with them, do not set foot on their paths;*

16 *for their feet rush into sin, they are swift to shed blood.*

17 *How useless to spread a net in full view of all the birds!*

18 *These men lie in wait for their own blood; they waylay only themselves!*

19 *Such is the end of all who go after ill-gotten gain; it takes away the lives of those who get it.*

20 *Wisdom calls aloud in the street, she raises her voice in the public squares;*

21 *at the head of the noisy streets she cries out, in the gateways of*
the city she makes her speech:
22 *How long will you simple ones love your simple ways? How*
long will mockers delight in mockery and fools hate knowledge?
23 *If you had responded to my rebuke, I would have poured out my*
heart to you and made my thoughts known to you.
24 *But since you rejected me when I called and no one gave heed*
when I stretched out my hand,
25 *since you ignored all my advice and would not accept my rebuke,*
26 *I in turn will laugh at your disaster; I will mock when calamity*
overtakes you—
27 *when calamity overtakes you like a storm, when disaster sweeps*
over you like a whirlwind, when distress and trouble overwhelm
you.
28 *"Then they will call to me but I will not answer; they will look for*
me but will not find me.
29 *Since they hated knowledge and did not choose to fear the* LORD,
30 *since they would not accept my advice and spurned my rebuke,*
31 *they will eat the fruit of their ways and be filled with the fruit of*
their schemes.
32 *For the waywardness of the simple will kill them, and the*
complacency of fools will destroy them;
33 *but whoever listens to me will live in safety and be at ease, without*
fear of harm."

CHAPTER 1

AN AWESOME GOD

Proverbs 1:1-33
Key verse: "The fear of the Lord..."
— Proverbs 1:7

Are you afraid of God?

Probably not, unless you were reared in a legalistic church as I was. The God of my adolescence was a cross between a medieval executioner and a hanging judge. He meted out judgment with sadistic delight and extended forgiveness grudgingly, and then only to the most penitent. The mere thought of Him caused me to tremble in terror. In truth, I feared Him, but I did not love Him.

As a young adult, I rejected the sadistic God of my adolescence. I simply could not live with the kind of fear and condemnation He generated in me. In His place I created a gracious heavenly Father, a God Who loved me unconditionally, One Who gladly forgave my sins. Here was a God I could love, but I did not revere Him.

Who is the real God — the stern and distant deity of my adolescent years, or the benevolent and kindly father figure with which I replaced Him? Neither? Both? To find the answer we must turn, not to our subjective experiences, but to the eternal Scriptures.

God, as He reveals Himself in Scripture, is altogether holy,[1] absolutely just[2] and totally righteous.[3] Because He is holy, He cannot tolerate sin. Being just, He cannot allow a single sinful act to go unpunished. And because He is righteous, He cannot fellowship with anyone who does not measure up to His holy standard. In addition, the Scriptures reveal that He is infinite, eternal and wholly unapproachable. No wonder the ancient Hebrews pleaded with Moses, "...'Speak to us yourself and we will listen. But do not have God speak to us or we will die.'"[4]

Yet, the Scriptures also declare that He is a God of love,[5] mercy[6] and grace.[7] Being a God of love, He cannot turn His back on fallen humanity without denying that part of His eternal character. And because He is a God of mercy and grace, He cannot allow mankind to be eternally lost without providing for our salvation.

Herein lies the dilemma — how can God be both just and merciful? How can He forgive our sins without betraying His justice? Yet, by the same token, if He does not forgive our sins, will He not betray His love and mercy?

Only the wisdom of God could find a solution, and only the love of God could make that solution a living reality. Through the incarnation of Jesus, the love and wisdom of God manifest themselves in glorious detail.

By becoming one of us and living a sinless life, Jesus fully satisfied the holy demands of a righteous God,[8] thus making it possible for God to accept us. Through His sacrificial death, Jesus suffered the full penalty for our sins, thus satisfying the just demands of a holy God, and making it possible for God to forgive our sins without violating His character. Since both His just and righteous demands have been satisfied, God is now free to manifest His love and mercy toward us.

So great is the love of God that there are times when I am tempted to make light of sin, to foolishly think that it is no big thing. Then I remember the Cross! That's what God thinks about sin. It is so deadly, so evil, that it must be dealt with even if it means punishing His own son. The prophet Isaiah says that Jesus was, "...stricken by God, smitten by him, and afflicted....it was the LORD's will to crush him and cause him to suffer....For he bore the sin of many...."[9]

And if ever I am tempted to doubt the love of God, to think that my repeated failures have driven me beyond the reach of His love, I remember the Cross! That's God's love message to me! With iron spikes, broken flesh and spilled blood He pours out His love for me — "But

God demonstrates his own love for us in this: While we were still sinners, Christ died for us."[10]

Truly this is a God I can both love and revere!

ACTION STEPS:

☐ Examine your image of God, your understanding of His character and nature. Make a list of His attributes.

☐ Now examine your list. Are the attributes you listed based on Scripture or are they a kind of composite sketch based on your own subjective experiences?

☐ Consciously ask God to reveal Himself to you so that you may love and revere Him as you should.

THOUGHT FOR THE DAY:

"'Fear' is best understood as 'reverent obedience.' Although it includes worship, it does not end there. It radiates out from our adoration and devotion to our everyday conduct that sees each moment as the Lord's time, each relationship as the Lord's opportunity, each duty as the Lord's command, and each blessing as the Lord's gift. It is a new way of looking at life and seeing what it is meant to be when viewed from God's perspective."[11]

— David A. Hubbard

PRAYER:

Lord, deliver me from my misconceptions. Let me know You as You truly are that I may worship You as I should. In the name of Jesus I pray. Amen.

PROVERBS 2

1 *My son, if you accept my words and store up my commands within you,*

2 *turning your ear to wisdom and applying your heart to understanding,*

3 *and if you call out for insight and cry aloud for understanding,*

4 *and if you look for it as for silver and search for it as for hidden treasure,*

5 *then you will understand the fear of the* LORD *and find the knowledge of God.*

6 *For the* LORD *gives wisdom, and from his mouth come knowledge and understanding.*

7 *He holds victory in store for the upright, he is a shield to those whose walk is blameless,*

8 *for he guards the course of the just and protects the way of his faithful ones.*

9 *Then you will understand what is right and just and fair—every good path.*

10 *For wisdom will enter your heart, and knowledge will be pleasant to your soul.*

11 *Discretion will protect you, and understanding will guard you.*

12 *Wisdom will save you from the ways of wicked men, from men whose words are perverse,*

13 *who leave the straight paths to walk in dark ways,*

14 *who delight in doing wrong and rejoice in the perverseness of evil,*

15 *whose paths are crooked and who are devious in their ways.*

16 *It will save you also from the adulteress, from the wayward wife with her seductive words,*

17 *who has left the partner of her youth and ignored the covenant she made before God.*

18 *For her house leads down to death and her paths to the spirits of the dead.*

19 *None who go to her return or attain the paths of life.*

20 *Thus you will walk in the ways of good men and keep to the paths of the righteous.*

PROVERBS 2

21 *For the upright will live in the land, and the blameless will remain in it;*

22 *but the wicked will be cut off from the land, and the unfaithful will be torn from it.*

CHAPTER 2

THE WISDOM OF GOD

Proverbs 2:1-22

Key verse: "For the Lord gives wisdom, and from his mouth come knowledge and understanding."
— Proverbs 2:6

The question before us is not, will the Lord give us wisdom? That's a given: "If any of you lacks wisdom, he should ask God, who gives generously to all...."[1] For us the question is, how does God impart His wisdom?

First, God reveals His wisdom through the Scriptures. They are filled with practical truths warning us against co-signing a note,[2] idleness,[3] reckless words,[4] selfishness,[5] dishonesty in business[6] and foolish companions,[7] to name just a few. They also provide great principles, eternal truths, which become the core values that govern our lives. Principles like: "...'seek first his [God's] kingdom and his righteousness, and all these things will be given to you as well.'"[8] Or, "'Whoever finds his life will lose it, and whoever loses his life for my [Jesus'] sake will find it.'"[9]

A second way that God imparts His wisdom is through others. Proverbs 13:20 declares, "He who walks with the wise grows wise, but a companion of fools suffers harm."

Some years ago a dear friend of mine went through an extremely difficult time. The congregation where he served as senior pastor was unusually critical and finally forced him to resign. Although this situation was extremely painful for him and his family, not to mention the financial adversity it created, he never uttered an unkind word.

One day, while we were having coffee, I asked him how he managed to maintain such a positive attitude and such a pure spirit. Without a moment's hesitation he replied, "I've never been a bitter or vindictive person, and I'm not going to let anyone make me something I'm not!"

In that instant I recognized that God was giving me special wisdom through the words and experience of my friend. Since that day I have had more than one occasion to act on the truth he imparted, and it has served me well, protecting me from the snare of the enemy.

A third way God imparts His wisdom is through the inner prompting of His Spirit. Throughout my years of ministry, I have faced a number of situations which were beyond my expertise. On such occasions I go to God in prayer. Like Solomon of old, I pray, "'Give me wisdom and knowledge, that I may lead this people....'"[10]

Without fail, God answers my desperate prayer. Sometimes He speaks to me from the Scriptures, or through the counsel of a trusted friend, but more often than not His wisdom comes as a thought, a solution, a course of action. And once conceived it often seems so simple, so obvious, that I am tempted to discount His role in it. Yet a more spiritually sensitive part of me recognizes it as the wisdom of God.

Usually God does not answer my prayer while I am praying. I mean, I often leave the place of prayer without a clue as to what to do. Most often the answer comes when I least expect it, when I am not even thinking about the problem. Sometimes it comes as my first thought upon awaking in the morning, full blown and complete. At other times it comes to me while I am showering or when I am driving. I can only conclude that my mind needs to be at rest before God can impart His wisdom to me.

ACTION STEPS:

☐ Recall a time when God imparted wisdom to you. How did He communicate it to you? Was it in one of the three ways I mentioned or in some other way?

☐ If you are facing a challenging situation or an important decision, surrender it to God in prayer right now. Ask Him to give you the wisdom to make a wise decision.

☐ Over the next several days be aware of the ways you receive input to resolve this situation. Be especially sensitive to the presence of God at work in your life and make note of it.

THOUGHT FOR THE DAY:

"When a pond is greatly agitated by the breezes and the wind, one can throw in a pebble or even many pebbles and there is no noticeable effect. When a pond is perfectly at peace and one casts a pebble into it, the gentle waves spread in every direction till they reach even the farthest shore. When we are in the midst of a busy everyday life, so many thoughts go in and out of our minds and our hearts, we don't perceive the effect they are having upon us. But when we come to achieve a deeper inner quiet, then we are much more discerning. The way is open to follow even the most gentle leadings of the Spirit and to avoid even the most subtle deviations that are suggested either by the self or by the evil one."[11]

— M. Basil Pennington

PRAYER:

Lord, still my overactive mind and quiet my rambunctious spirit. Make me sensitive to the gentle prompting of Your Spirit that I may know and do Your will. In the name of Jesus I pray. Amen.

PROVERBS 3

1 *My son, do not forget my teaching, but keep my commands in your heart,*

2 *for they will prolong your life many years and bring you prosperity.*

3 *Let love and faithfulness never leave you; bind them around your neck, write them on the tablet of your heart.*

4 *Then you will win favor and a good name in the sight of God and man.*

5 *Trust in the* LORD *with all your heart and lean not on your own understanding;*

6 *in all your ways acknowledge him, and he will make your paths straight.*

7 *Do not be wise in your own eyes; fear the* LORD *and shun evil.*

8 *This will bring health to your body and nourishment to your bones.*

9 *Honor the* LORD *with your wealth, with the firstfruits of all your crops;*

10 *then your barns will be filled to overflowing, and your vats will brim over with new wine.*

11 *My son, do not despise the* LORD*'s discipline and do not resent his rebuke,*

12 *because the* LORD *disciplines those he loves, as a father the son he delights in.*

13 *Blessed is the man who finds wisdom, the man who gains understanding,*

14 *for she is more profitable than silver and yields better returns than gold.*

15 *She is more precious than rubies; nothing you desire can compare with her.*

16 *Long life is in her right hand; in her left hand are riches and honor.*

17 *Her ways are pleasant ways, and all her paths are peace.*

18 *She is a tree of life to those who embrace her; those who lay hold of her will be blessed.*

19 *By wisdom the* LORD *laid the earth's foundations, by understanding he set the heavens in place;*

20 *by his knowledge the deeps were divided, and the clouds let drop the dew.*

PROVERBS 3

21 *My son, preserve sound judgment and discernment, do not let them out of your sight;*

22 *they will be life for you, an ornament to grace your neck.*

23 *Then you will go on your way in safety, and your foot will not stumble;*

24 *when you lie down, you will not be afraid; when you lie down, your sleep will be sweet.*

25 *Have no fear of sudden disaster or of the ruin that overtakes the wicked,*

26 *for the* LORD *will be your confidence and will keep your foot from being snared.*

27 *Do not withhold good from those who deserve it, when it is in your power to act.*

28 *Do not say to your neighbor, "Come back later; I'll give it tomorrow"— when you now have it with you.*

29 *Do not plot harm against your neighbor, who lives trustfully near you.*

30 *Do not accuse a man for no reason — when he has done you no harm.*

31 *Do not envy a violent man or choose any of his ways,*

32 *for the* LORD *detests a perverse man but takes the upright into his confidence.*

33 *The* LORD*'s curse is on the house of the wicked, but he blesses the home of the righteous.*

34 *He mocks proud mockers but gives grace to the humble.*

35 *The wise inherit honor, but fools he holds up to shame.*

CHAPTER 3

GOD'S WHEELBARROW

Proverbs 3:1-35

Key verses: "Trust in the Lord with all your heart and lean not on your own understanding; in all your ways acknowledge him, and he will make your paths straight."

— Proverbs 3:5,6

Undoubtedly, you are familiar with the story of the high-wire artist who announced that he was going to cross Niagara Falls on a tightrope pushing a wheelbarrow. The scheduled day finally arrived, and hundreds of people gathered to witness his daring feat. With bated breath they watched him make his torturous journey, and when he finally reached the safety of the far shore, they roared their approval.

As he prepared for his return trip, he asked the crowd if they believed he could do it again. They responded enthusiastically. To a man, they believed he could do it. Raising his hands for silence he asked, "Do you believe I can do it with a man in the wheelbarrow?" With a single voice they shouted, "You can do it!"

Once more he quieted the crowd and when he had their attention he asked for a volunteer. A somber silence settled over the crowd; a few whispered among themselves, but no one stepped forward. It was soon apparent that, while no one doubted that he could do it, neither did anyone trust him enough to get in the wheelbarrow.

When the wise man exhorts us to "Trust in the Lord with all [our] heart..."[1] he is not talking about the kind of trust that stands in the crowd and cheers. Rather the trust he's writing about is active. It dares to risk everything, dares to climb in God's "wheelbarrow."

Well do I remember when God asked me to trust Him with my writing career. At the time I had been writing for twelve years and had published two books and scores of articles. Now God was asking me to give up my writing to concentrate on my duties as senior pastor. For the next seven years I did not write a single thing for publication, and as far as I knew, I might never write again. With a single-minded obedience, I devoted all of my energies to the church.

It didn't make sense to me. At nineteen I had been called by God to write, and it was obvious that He had given me a talent for it. Why then, would He ask me to give it up? Still, I made a decision to trust the Lord rather than my own understanding. With that decision, I found the strength to give up my dreams of being an author.

From time to time the itch to write returned, but each time it did I surrendered it to the Lord once again. After a while I was even able to make peace with my decision. My writing, like the rest of my life, was now in God's hands. In His time, I believed, He would release me to write again; but if He did not, then I would trust His wisdom.

Imagine my joy when Honor Books approached me in the spring of 1987. After several meetings and three weeks of prayer (I had to be sure that this was God's doing and not just an elaborate temptation), I felt released of the Lord to write again. With great joy I returned to my writing, and in the past seven years I have written ten books. With the wise man I can say, "In everything you do, put God first, and he will direct you and crown your efforts with success."[2]

ACTION STEPS:

☐ Examine your heart and life to see if you are trusting in the Lord with all of your heart. Have you placed your life, your family, your career, in God's "wheelbarrow"?

☐ If you have not put everything in God's "wheelbarrow," make a decision to do so right now. Be sensitive to the thoughts and impressions that come to you as you wait quietly before the Lord. Be obedient to His guidance even if it isn't easy.

☐ Share your decision with your pastor or a trusted Christian friend.

THOUGHT FOR THE DAY:

"I am afraid of saying 'Yes,' Lord.
Where will you take me?
I am afraid of drawing the long straw,
I am afraid of signing my name to an
unread agreement,
I am afraid of the 'yes' that entails other 'yeses.'

"O Lord, I am afraid of your demands, but who can resist you?
That your Kingdom may come and not mine,
That your will may be done and not mine,
Help me to say 'Yes.'"[3]

— Michel Quoist

PRAYER:

Lord, teach me to trust You with the daily events of my life, the little things, the mundane details, that I may have the courage to trust You with the really important things. In the name of Jesus I pray. Amen.

PROVERBS 4

1 *Listen, my sons, to a father's instruction; pay attention and gain understanding.*

2 *I give you sound learning, so do not forsake my teaching.*

3 *When I was a boy in my father's house, still tender, and an only child of my mother,*

4 *he taught me and said, "Lay hold of my words with all your heart; keep my commands and you will live.*

5 *Get wisdom, get understanding; do not forget my words or swerve from them.*

6 *Do not forsake wisdom, and she will protect you; love her, and she will watch over you.*

7 *Wisdom is supreme; therefore get wisdom. Though it cost all you have, get understanding.*

8 *Esteem her, and she will exalt you; embrace her, and she will honor you.*

9 *She will set a garland of grace on your head and present you with a crown of splendor."*

10 *Listen, my son, accept what I say, and the years of your life will be many.*

11 *I guide you in the way of wisdom and lead you along straight paths.*

12 *When you walk, your steps will not be hampered; when you run, you will not stumble.*

13 *Hold on to instruction, do not let it go; guard it well, for it is your life.*

14 *Do not set foot on the path of the wicked or walk in the way of evil men.*

15 *Avoid it, do not travel on it; turn from it and go on your way.*

16 *For they cannot sleep till they do evil; they are robbed of slumber till they make someone fall.*

17 *They eat the bread of wickedness and drink the wine of violence.*

18 *The path of the righteous is like the first gleam of dawn, shining ever brighter till the full light of day.*

19 *But the way of the wicked is like deep darkness; they do not know what makes them stumble.*

PROVERBS 4

20 *My son, pay attention to what I say; listen closely to my words.*

21 *Do not let them out of your sight, keep them within your heart;*

22 *for they are life to those who find them and health to a man's whole body.*

23 *Above all else, guard your heart, for it is the wellspring of life.*

24 *Put away perversity from your mouth; keep corrupt talk far from your lips.*

25 *Let your eyes look straight ahead, fix your gaze directly before you.*

26 *Make level paths for your feet and take only ways that are firm.*

27 *Do not swerve to the right or the left; keep your foot from evil.*

CHAPTER 4

MATTERS OF THE HEART

Proverbs 4:1-27

Key verse: "Above all else, guard your heart, for it is the wellspring of life."

— Proverbs 4:23

When the Scriptures speak of the heart, they are not referring to the physical organ that circulates blood through the body. Rather, they are referring to the core of an individual's being, who he is as a person. In biblical language, the heart is the source of emotions, the fountainhead of thoughts and desires, the motivating force in life.

All that a man does, whether good or evil, originates in his heart. Jesus said, "A good man out of the good treasure of the heart bringeth forth good things: and an evil man out of the evil treasure bringeth forth evil things."[1] Nowhere is this truth more clearly seen than in the life of John Hinkley, Jr. — the man who shot President Ronald Reagan.

In the weeks following his unsuccessful assassination attempt, the bizarre story behind his crime became clear. According to the FBI, Hinkley was acting out a romantic fantasy involving Hollwood actress Jody Foster. His fantasy was a takeoff on the movie *Taxi Driver* in which Foster played a young prostitute pursued by a love-crazed cabby. In a desperate attempt to win her love, the cabby assassinated a government official. Apparently, the deeply disturbed Hinkley thought he could win Foster's love by assassinating the president of the United States.

While the Hinkley case is extreme, to be sure, it is also classic. It graphically demonstrates the connection between a person's secret thoughts, his deepest feelings and his actions. The implications are clear: think on something long enough — fantasize about it, feed it — and it will ultimately become overpowering!

While most of us will never fantasize about killing the president of the United States, our secret desires are just as prophetic. Inevitably, the thoughts and feelings we harbor in our hearts become the attitudes and actions of our lives. Early on, they are just seeds scattered across the soil of our heart. With a minimum of effort we can sweep them away; but if we delay, or worse yet, if we nurture them, they will take root. Even then, we can uproot them; but if we do not act quickly, they will overwhelm us.

Many a man has mistakenly assumed that he could reserve a part of his heart for weeds, only to discover that evil is a malignancy that invades every part of his being. In time its roots reach even into the most sacred areas of his life, choking out all that is good and decent. Ultimately, he finds himself behaving in ways that were once unthinkable to him. No wonder the wise man writes, "Above all else, guard your heart, for it is the wellspring of life."[2]

ACTION STEPS:

☐ Take an inventory of your heart. Are you harboring any unclean thoughts or feelings? Things like resentment, jealousy, lust or anger?

☐ Pray Psalm 139:23,24: "Search me, O God, and know my heart; test me and know my anxious thoughts. See if there is any offensive way in me, and lead me in the way everlasting."

☐ Pray Psalm 51:10: "Create in me a pure heart, O God, and renew a steadfast spirit within me."

THOUGHT FOR THE DAY:

"Almost every personal defeat begins with our failure to know ourselves, to have a clear view of our capabilities (negative and positive), our propensities, our weak sides."[3]

— Gordon MacDonald

"The Bible characters never fell on their weak points but on their strong ones; unguarded strength is double weakness."[4]

— Oswald Chambers

PRAYER:

Lord, create in me a clean heart, a pure heart, and fill it with Your love and goodness. Heal my wounded spirit and deliver me from the old hurts that I have so carefully kept. Free me from the envy and jealousy that have taken root in my soul. Now set a watch over my heart, lest any unclean thing take root there. In the name of Jesus I pray. Amen.

PROVERBS 5

1 *My son, pay attention to my wisdom, listen well to my words of insight,*

2 *that you may maintain discretion and your lips may preserve knowledge.*

3 *For the lips of an adulteress drip honey, and her speech is smoother than oil;*

4 *but in the end she is bitter as gall, sharp as a double-edged sword.*

5 *Her feet go down to death; her steps lead straight to the grave.*

6 *She gives no thought to the way of life; her paths are crooked, but she knows it not.*

7 *Now then, my sons, listen to me; do not turn aside from what I say.*

8 *Keep to a path far from her, do not go near the door of her house,*

9 *lest you give your best strength to others and your years to one who is cruel,*

10 *lest strangers feast on your wealth and your toil enrich another man's house.*

11 *At the end of your life you will groan, when your flesh and body are spent.*

12 *You will say, "How I hated discipline! How my heart spurned correction!*

13 *I would not obey my teachers or listen to my instructors.*

14 *I have come to the brink of utter ruin in the midst of the whole assembly."*

15 *Drink water from your own cistern, running water from your own well.*

16 *Should your springs overflow in the streets, your streams of water in the public squares?*

17 *Let them be yours alone, never to be shared with strangers.*

18 *May your fountain be blessed, and may you rejoice in the wife of your youth.*

19 *A loving doe, a graceful deer— may her breasts satisfy you always, may you ever be captivated by her love.*

20 *Why be captivated, my son, by an adulteress? Why embrace the bosom of another man's wife?*

PROVERBS 5

21 *For a man's ways are in full view of the* LORD, *and he examines all his paths.*
22 *The evil deeds of a wicked man ensnare him; the cords of his sin hold him fast.*
23 *He will die for lack of discipline, led astray by his own great folly.*

CHAPTER 5

FATAL ATTRACTION

Proverbs 5:1-23

Key verses: "For the lips of an adulteress drip honey, and her speech is smoother than oil; but in the end she is bitter as gall, sharp as a double-edged sword. Her feet go down to death; her steps lead straight to the grave."

— Proverbs 5:3-5

Contrary to popular myth, the way to a man's heart is not through his stomach, but through his ego. Let a woman flatter him, make him feel important, indispensable, irresistible, and he will follow her anywhere, even to the doorway of death.

"With persuasive words" the wise man writes, "she led him astray; she seduced him with her smooth talk....he followed her like an ox going to the slaughter....little knowing it will cost him his life."[1]

Once an adulterous relationship begins, it is almost impossible to break it off. Compared to illicit sex, married love can seem dull and uninteresting. It isn't, of course, but in the heat and excitement of an affair, it can seem that way. Extramarital sex confuses excitement (lust) with love, and married sex can never satisfy the unfaithful heart's insatiable desire for illicit excitement. Hence the "fatal attraction."

There are moments of sinful pleasure, to be sure — the excitement of the hunt, the thrill of the conquest — but the end is death.

Death to the adulterer's relationship with God, for his sin separates him from fellowship with the Lord. Like Adam, after he had partaken of the forbidden fruit, the adulterer ends up dreading God's nearness and looking for some place where he can hide from His holy love. For a while he may maintain a spiritual facade, he may even fool his friends and family, but at the core of his being he is dead! Where once there burned a holy fire, now there is only ashes.

Death to the adulterer's marriage, for even if he manages to keep the facts of his adultery secret, his very secrecy will rob his marriage of its intimacy, its life. And more likely than not, his adultery will become common knowledge, severely wounding, not only his wife, but his children as well.

Adultery also signals the death of the adulterer's self-respect, for he has betrayed his own values. Even if no one else ever finds out, he knows. He knows that he is not the faithful husband and godly father he appears to be. He is not the spiritual leader or the man of integrity his friends think he is. As one adulterer so poignantly put it, "It's a terrible thing to know that you are not the man your family and friends think you are."

Yet, as tragic as adultery is, the grace of God is greater still: "'...God does not take away life; instead, he devises ways so that a banished person may not remain estranged from him.'"[2] Through the sacrificial death of Jesus Christ, God has made a way to forgive the adulterer and to reconcile him to Himself.

"'Come now, let us reason together,' says the Lord. 'Though your sins are like scarlet, they shall be as white as snow; though they are red as crimson, they shall be like wool.'"[3]

ACTION STEPS:

☐ Examine your relationships. Is your marriage in good repair? Are you giving it the time and attention it requires? Are you currently involved in any friendship that you cannot tell your pastor and your wife about?

☐ If you are involved in any kind of inappropriate relationship — even if it is not yet adultery — confess it to the Lord and receive His forgiveness. Then make yourself accountable to your pastor or a trusted Christian brother.

☐ With the help of your pastor or a Christian brother make a list of guidelines for all future relationships.

THOUGHT FOR THE DAY:

"If we refuse to take the fact of sin into our calculation, refuse to agree that a base impulse runs through men, that there is such a thing as vice and self-seeking, when our hour of darkness strikes, instead of being acquainted with sin and the grief of it, we will compromise straight away...."[4]

— Oswald Chambers

PRAYER:

Lord, don't let me get away with denying my sexual desires or with pretending that I am not tempted. Instead, teach me to honestly evaluate my weaknesses and to take appropriate steps to guard myself. Redeem my sexual desires, sanctify them, make them a pure and holy gift to my wife. In the name of Jesus I pray. Amen.

PROVERBS 6

1 *My son, if you have put up security for your neighbor, if you have struck hands in pledge for another,*

2 *if you have been trapped by what you said, ensnared by the words of your mouth,*

3 *then do this, my son, to free yourself, since you have fallen into your neighbor's hands: Go and humble yourself; press your plea with your neighbor!*

4 *Allow no sleep to your eyes, no slumber to your eyelids.*

5 *Free yourself, like a gazelle from the hand of the hunter, like a bird from the snare of the fowler.*

6 *Go to the ant, you sluggard; consider its ways and be wise!*

7 *It has no commander, no overseer or ruler,*

8 *yet it stores its provisions in summer and gathers its food at harvest.*

9 *How long will you lie there, you sluggard? When will you get up from your sleep?*

10 *A little sleep, a little slumber, a little folding of the hands to rest—*

11 *and poverty will come on you like a bandit and scarcity like an armed man.*

12 *A scoundrel and villain, who goes about with a corrupt mouth,*

13 *who winks with his eye, signals with his feet and motions with his fingers,*

14 *who plots evil with deceit in his heart — he always stirs up dissension.*

15 *Therefore disaster will overtake him in an instant; he will suddenly be destroyed—without remedy.*

16 *There are six things the* LORD *hates, seven that are detestable to him:*

17 *haughty eyes, a lying tongue, hands that shed innocent blood,*

18 *a heart that devises wicked schemes, feet that are quick to rush into evil,*

19 *a false witness who pours out lies and a man who stirs up dissension among brothers.*

20 *My son, keep your father's commands and do not forsake your mother's teaching.*

PROVERBS 6

21 *Bind them upon your heart forever; fasten them around your neck.*

22 *When you walk, they will guide you; when you sleep, they will watch over you; when you awake, they will speak to you.*

23 *For these commands are a lamp, this teaching is a light, and the corrections of discipline are the way to life,*

24 *keeping you from the immoral woman, from the smooth tongue of the wayward wife.*

25 *Do not lust in your heart after her beauty or let her captivate you with her eyes,*

26 *for the prostitute reduces you to a loaf of bread, and the adulteress preys upon your very life.*

27 *Can a man scoop fire into his lap without his clothes being burned?*

28 *Can a man walk on hot coals without his feet being scorched?*

29 *So is he who sleeps with another man's wife; no one who touches her will go unpunished.*

30 *Men do not despise a thief if he steals to satisfy his hunger when he is starving.*

31 *Yet if he is caught, he must pay sevenfold, though it costs him all the wealth of his house.*

32 *But a man who commits adultery lacks judgment; whoever does so destroys himself.*

33 *Blows and disgrace are his lot, and his shame will never be wiped away;*

34 *for jealousy arouses a husband's fury, and he will show no mercy when he takes revenge.*

35 *He will not accept any compensation; he will refuse the bribe, however great it is.*

CHAPTER 6

From Riches to Rags

Proverbs 6:1-35

Key verses: "Go to the ant, you sluggard; consider its ways and be wise! It has no commander, no overseer or ruler, yet it stores its provisions in summer and gathers its food at harvest. How long will you lie there, you sluggard? When will you get up from your sleep? A little sleep, a little slumber, a little folding of the hands to rest — and poverty will come on you like a bandit and scarcity like an armed man."

— Proverbs 6:6-11

Financial failure is devastating, especially when it involves not only the loss of a business, but the repossession of a person's home and autos as well. In truth, few experiences in life are more humiliating to a man. It strikes at the very core of his being, of his manhood. To him it is evidence that he has failed in his primary responsibility of providing for his wife and children.

Over the years, I've walked through this painful scenario with more than one man. Although each experience is unique, they do have some things in common. In such situations, most men experience a time of depression followed by a period of intense introspection. Those who are able to honestly examine their failure often recover and go on to experience success in business. On the other hand, those whose introspection is designed only to find a scapegoat usually end up feeling victimized and seemed doomed to fail again.

Not infrequently, the root cause is nothing more than outright laziness — what used to be called slothfulness. It manifests itself in a number of different ways. Inattention to details is one. Refusing to do the grunt work that assures success is another. Staying busy without being productive — using busy work to avoid dealing with real issues — is a third. Another common manifestation of slothfulness is the "working lunch," what is commonly referred to as "developing contacts." Finally, there is the "big deal" syndrome. The man caught in this trap is self-deceived. He can't be bothered with making a living or building a business. All of his time and energy is devoted to closing the "big deal," the one that is going to make him an instant millionaire.

"Go to the ant," counsels the ancient sage, "...consider its ways and be wise! It has no commander, no overseer or ruler, yet it stores its provisions in summer and gathers its food at harvest."[1]

From the ant we learn to be self-starters. It doesn't need to be motivated by another; it has no foreman or supervisor. Although it is tiny, and of primitive intelligence, it still has the good sense to work hard and plan ahead. Because it gathers and stores its provisions in the summer, it has plenty when the barrenness of winter comes.

The lazy person, on the other hand, can find a hundred and one excuses for not working. "The sluggard says, 'There is a lion outside!' or, 'I will be murdered in the streets!'"[2] Nor is he open to counsel: "The sluggard is wiser in his own eyes than seven men who answer discreetly."[3]

As a consequence, he is doomed to repeat his mistakes and to suffer repeatedly the accompanying consequences. "I went past the field of the sluggard, past the vineyard of the man who lacks judgment; thorns had come up everywhere, the ground was covered with weeds, and the stone wall was in ruins. I applied my heart to what I observed and learned a lesson from what I saw: A little sleep, a little slumber, a little folding of the hands to rest — and poverty will come on you like a bandit and scarcity like an armed man."[4]

Remember, God will not prosper a lazy person. He blesses the work of our hands, not our idleness.[5] "The sluggard craves and gets nothing, but the desires of the diligent are fully satisfied."[6]

ACTION STEPS:

☐ Examine your work habits. Are you conscientious? Do you do more than is expected of you? Do you take pride in your work, even the mundane details?

☐ If you are a diligent and conscientious worker, see if you can determine the source of your work ethic. Did it come from your parents, from a teacher or a mentor, or from some other source?

☐ If you sense a need for improvement in your job performance, specifically list three or four changes that you are going to make.

☐ Now consciously choose to see your work as a worship gift which you offer daily to the Lord.

THOUGHT FOR THE DAY:

"We do not consider manual work as a curse, or a bitter necessity, not even as a means of making a living. We consider it as a high human function. As a basis of human life. The most dignified thing in the life of a human being and which ought to be free, creative. Men ought to be proud of it."[7]

—David Ben-Gurion

PRAYER:

Lord, I thank You for physical strength and the ability to work. I thank You for using my work as a means of providing for my wife and children. Let my work be a blessing, not only to my employer, but also to all those who benefit from what I produce. Bless now the work of my hands this day and every day. In the name of Jesus I pray. Amen.

PROVERBS 7

1 *My son, keep my words and store up my commands within you.*

2 *Keep my commands and you will live; guard my teachings as the apple of your eye.*

3 *Bind them on your fingers; write them on the tablet of your heart.*

4 *Say to wisdom, "You are my sister," and call understanding your kinsman;*

5 *they will keep you from the adulteress, from the wayward wife with her seductive words.*

6 *At the window of my house I looked out through the lattice.*

7 *I saw among the simple, I noticed among the young men, a youth who lacked judgment.*

8 *He was going down the street near her corner, walking along in the direction of her house*

9 *at twilight, as the day was fading, as the dark of night set in.*

10 *Then out came a woman to meet him, dressed like a prostitute and with crafty intent.*

11 *(She is loud and defiant, her feet never stay at home;*

12 *now in the street, now in the squares, at every corner she lurks.)*

13 *She took hold of him and kissed him and with a brazen face she said:*

14 *"I have fellowship offerings at home; today I fulfilled my vows.*

15 *So I came out to meet you; I looked for you and have found you!*

16 *I have covered my bed with colored linens from Egypt.*

17 *I have perfumed my bed with myrrh, aloes and cinnamon.*

18 *Come, let's drink deep of love till morning; let's enjoy ourselves with love!*

19 *My husband is not at home; he has gone on a long journey.*

20 *He took his purse filled with money and will not be home till full moon."*

21 *With persuasive words she led him astray; she seduced him with her smooth talk.*

22 *All at once he followed her like an ox going to the slaughter, like a deer stepping into a noose*

PROVERBS 7

23 *till an arrow pierces his liver, like a bird darting into a snare, little knowing it will cost him his life.*

24 *Now then, my sons, listen to me; pay attention to what I say.*

25 *Do not let your heart turn to her ways or stray into her paths.*

26 *Many are the victims she has brought down; her slain are a mighty throng.*

27 *Her house is a highway to the grave, leading down to the chambers of death.*

CHAPTER 7

COUNT THE COST

Proverbs 7:1-27

Key verses: "My son, keep my words and store up my commands within you. Keep my commands and you will live; guard my teachings as the apple of your eye. Bind them on your fingers; write them on the tablet of your heart...they will keep you from the adulteress, from the wayward wife with her seductive words."

— Proverbs 7:1-3,5

I hung up the telephone in a daze. A member of our congregation had just been arrested for soliciting a prostitute who turned out to be an undercover police officer. I was shocked — there must be some mistake. I was angry — how could he do this to his wife and children, to his church, to me? I was deeply disappointed; I was grieved in my spirit.

And I was afraid. For months the national news had been filled with the tragic details of moral failure at the highest levels of the Church. As bad as that was, this was somehow worse. Those who had fallen were household names, to be sure, but this struck closer to home. Fearfully, I found myself wondering where it would end, wondering if anyone was safe from the enemy's snares.

Like a siren in the night, that tragic telephone call set off an alarm in my spirit. I could no longer pretend that it was only "bad" men who committed sexual sins. Evidence to the contrary was simply too compelling. Reluctantly, I concluded that a man cannot live in our sexually satiated society and long escape sexual temptation. Instead, he must prepare for it, he must be equipped to overcome it.

As I prayed and searched the Scriptures, the Lord revealed some principles which, if adhered to, will enable a man to overcome sexual temptation.

Principle #1: Listen to the counsel of godly men. "My son, keep my words and store up my commands within you...they will keep you from the adulteress, from the wayward wife with her seductive words."[1]

Principle #2: Make a covenant with your eyes. On the eve of his wedding, one young man asked me how he could be sure that he would never find a woman he desired more than his wife. My advice to him was simple: "Stop looking!"

Let Job be your example. He, "'...made a covenant with [his] eyes not to look lustfully at a girl.'"[2] The man who is serious about avoiding sexual sin will not window shop. He will have eyes only for his wife.

Principle #3: Guard your thought life. Most sexual sin begins in the imagination. Temptation comes first as a thought, then it becomes a desire. *The Living Bible* says, "Temptation is the pull of man's own evil thoughts and wishes. These evil thoughts lead to evil actions...."[3]

Sexually explicit thoughts are usually involuntary, at least initially. How a man handles these involuntary thoughts determines whether they become sin or not. If he welcomes such thoughts and embellishes them, they become sin. If he immediately repudiates them, they remain nothing more than temptation. As someone has said, "A man can't keep the birds from flying over his head, but he can stop them from building a nest in his hair."

Principle #4: Count the cost. Do you think for a moment that King David would have committed adultery with Bathsheba if he had stopped to count the cost? Would he have considered the sexual pleasures of a stolen night worth the lifetime of sorrow he suffered? I think not.

God forgave David,[4] to be sure, and we remember him, not as an adulterer, but as a man after God's own heart. Unfortunately, life was not so merciful. David's sin set in motion a tragic series of events that nearly destroyed his family and his kingdom.

The child born from his illicit union with Bathsheba dies suddenly from a mysterious illness. Amnon, David's son, rapes his sister Tamar, creating a scandal in the palace. Two years later, Tamar's brother Absalom takes his revenge and murders Amnon. Finally, Absalom leads an armed rebellion against his father David, driving him from Jerusalem and breaking his heart. And on the rooftop of the palace where David first lusted after Bathsheba, Absalom pitches a tent and "...[lies] with his father's concubines in the sight of all Israel."[5]

This tragic account is included in Scripture, not to satisfy some prurient curiosity we might have, but as a warning lest we make the same mistake.[6] Remember, no one lives in a vacuum. A man's sinful decisions will affect not only himself, but everyone he loves and cares about. Yes, God will forgive our sins, but how much better to allow Him to deliver us from temptation before we sin.

ACTION STEPS:

☐ Think of the people you know who have committed sexual sin. Now consider the consequences they have suffered — things like guilt, regret, shame, loss of position, divorce, financial setback and sexually transmitted disease.

☐ Memorize Proverbs 6:32: "But a man who commits adultery lacks judgment; whoever does so destroys himself."

THOUGHT FOR THE DAY:

"A chain of seemingly innocent choices became destructive, and it was my fault. Choice by choice by choice, each easier to make, each becoming gradually darker. And then my world broke — in the very area I had predicted I was safe...."[7]

— Gordon MacDonald

PRAYER:

Lord, don't let me get away with any self-deceptive rationalization. Confront me, in my heart of hearts, with the truth about my relationships. Convict me of my sinful desires — uproot them. Deliver me from temptation, lest in my selfishness I destroy myself and those I love. In the name of Jesus I pray. Amen.

PROVERBS 8

1 *Does not wisdom call out? Does not understanding raise her voice?*
2 *On the heights along the way, where the paths meet, she takes her stand;*
3 *beside the gates leading into the city, at the entrances, she cries aloud:*
4 *To you, O men, I call out; I raise my voice to all mankind.*
5 *You who are simple, gain prudence; you who are foolish, gain understanding.*
6 *Listen, for I have worthy things to say; I open my lips to speak what is right.*
7 *My mouth speaks what is true, for my lips detest wickedness.*
8 *All the words of my mouth are just; none of them is crooked or perverse.*
9 *To the discerning all of them are right; they are faultless to those who have knowledge.*
10 *Choose my instruction instead of silver, knowledge rather than choice gold,*
11 *for wisdom is more precious than rubies, and nothing you desire can compare with her.*
12 *I, wisdom, dwell together with prudence; I possess knowledge and discretion.*
13 *To fear the* LORD *is to hate evil; I hate pride and arrogance, evil behavior and perverse speech.*
14 *Counsel and sound judgment are mine; I have understanding and power.*
15 *By me kings reign and rulers make laws that are just;*
16 *by me princes govern, and all nobles who rule on earth.*
17 *I love those who love me, and those who seek me find me.*
18 *With me are riches and honor, enduring wealth and prosperity.*
19 *My fruit is better than fine gold; what I yield surpasses choice silver.*
20 *I walk in the way of righteousness, along the paths of justice,*
21 *bestowing wealth on those who love me and making their treasuries full.*

PROVERBS 8

22 *"The* LORD *brought me forth as the first of his works,*
before his deeds of old;

23 *I was appointed from eternity, from the beginning, before the*
world began.

24 *When there were no oceans, I was given birth, when there were no*
springs abounding with water;

25 *before the mountains were settled in place, before the hills, I was*
given birth,

26 *before he made the earth or its fields or any of the dust of the*
world.

27 *I was there when he set the heavens in place, when he marked out*
the horizon on the face of the deep,

28 *when he established the clouds above and fixed securely the*
fountains of the deep,

29 *when he gave the sea its boundary so the waters would not*
overstep his command, and when he marked out the foundations of
the earth.

30 *Then I was the craftsman at his side. I was filled with delight day*
after day, rejoicing always in his presence,

31 *rejoicing in his whole world and delighting in mankind.*

32 *Now then, my sons, listen to me; blessed are those who keep my*
ways.

33 *Listen to my instruction and be wise; do not ignore it.*

34 *Blessed is the man who listens to me, watching daily at my doors,*
waiting at my doorway.

35 *For whoever finds me finds life and receives favor from the* LORD.

36 *But whoever fails to find me harms himself; all who hate me love*
death."

CHAPTER 8

SOLOMON'S CHOICE

Proverbs 8:1-36

Key verses: " 'To you, O men, I call out; I raise my voice to all mankind. You who are simple, gain prudence; you who are foolish, gain understanding...Choose my instruction instead of silver, knowledge rather than choice gold, for wisdom is more precious than rubies, and nothing you desire can compare with her....For whoever finds [wisdom] finds life and receives favor from the Lord.' "

— Proverbs 8:4,5,10,11,35

When Solomon penned these words, he was most likely at the height of his fame. As the king of Israel, he was the most powerful ruler in the world. His wealth and wisdom were legendary, inspiring visits from all manner of foreign dignitaries,[1] including the queen of Sheba.[2] Young men who aspired to royal service looked up to him as their model. Scholars suggest that his proverbs were created as curriculum for their training. That being the case, the most important thing he could impart to them was the secret of his success.

As he pondered that responsibility, perhaps his thoughts returned to his own beginnings, to the time God appeared to him in a dream: "...God said, 'Ask for whatever you want me to give you.' "[3]

With insight beyond his years, Solomon asked, not for riches or power, but for wisdom. This pleased the Lord, and He said, " '...I will give you a wise and discerning heart, so that there will never have been anyone like you, nor will there ever be. Moreover, I will give you what you have not asked for — both riches and honor — so that in your lifetime you will have no equal among kings.' "[4]

The wisdom Solomon received was a composite — "'...a discerning heart to govern...and to distinguish between right and wrong....'"[5] Nor was it long before his wisdom was put to the test. Two prostitutes came before him in a dispute about a baby. The facts were plain enough — each of them was the mother of a newborn infant. During the night one of the babies had died. Now both women were claiming the living child as her own. There were no witnesses. It was one mother's word against the other's.

"Then the king said,...'Cut the living child in two and give half to one and half to the other.'

"The woman whose son was alive was filled with compassion for her son and said to the king, 'Please, my lord, give her the living baby! Don't kill him!'...

"Then the king gave his ruling: 'Give the living baby to the first woman. Do not kill him; she is his mother.'

"When all Israel heard the verdict the king had given, they held the king in awe, because they saw that he had wisdom from God to administer justice."[6]

Inspired, perhaps by such memories, Solomon counsels the young men of his day, "'Choose my instruction instead of silver, knowledge rather than choice gold, for wisdom is more precious than rubies, and nothing you desire can compare with her....For whoever finds [wisdom] finds life and receives favor from the Lord.'"[7]

As men charged with the responsibility to lead our families, our churches and our communities, we too are in need of this wisdom from above. Thankfully, God has promised it to every man who asks.[8]

ACTION STEPS:

☐ Identify someone in your circle of friends or associates who demonstrates godly wisdom. Why did you choose this particular person? What character traits or actions caused you to conclude that he was a wise man? Be specific.

☐ If possible, arrange to have lunch or to go for coffee with this man. Share this chapter with him and ask him how he makes wise decisions. Ask him who was his mentor or model.

☐ Following your meeting, make a list of the things you learned and plan specific ways to integrate these principles into your own life.

THOUGHT FOR THE DAY:

"Wisdom is your perspective on life, your sense of balance, your understanding of how the various parts and principles apply and relate to each other. It embraces judgment, discernment, comprehension. It is a gestalt or oneness, an integrated wholeness."[9]

— Stephen R. Covey

PRAYER:

Lord, give me the desire to seek Your wisdom and the discipline to do those things that will prepare me to receive it. In the name of Jesus I pray. Amen.

PROVERBS 9

1 *Wisdom has built her house; she has hewn out its seven pillars.*
2 *She has prepared her meat and mixed her wine; she has also set her table.*
3 *She has sent out her maids, and she calls from the highest point of the city.*
4 *"Let all who are simple come in here!" she says to those who lack judgment.*
5 *"Come, eat my food and drink the wine I have mixed.*
6 *Leave your simple ways and you will live; walk in the way of understanding.*
7 *Whoever corrects a mocker invites insult; whoever rebukes a wicked man incurs abuse.*
8 *Do not rebuke a mocker or he will hate you; rebuke a wise man and he will love you.*
9 *Instruct a wise man and he will be wiser still; teach a righteous man and he will add to his learning.*
10 *The fear of the* LORD *is the beginning of wisdom, and knowledge of the Holy One is understanding.*
11 *For through me your days will be many, and years will be added to your life.*
12 *If you are wise, your wisdom will reward you; if you are a mocker, you alone will suffer."*
13 *The woman Folly is loud; she is undisciplined and without knowledge.*
14 *She sits at the door of her house, on a seat at the highest point of the city,*
15 *calling out to those who pass by, who go straight on their way.*
16 *"Let all who are simple come in here!" she says to those who lack judgment.*
17 *"Stolen water is sweet; food eaten in secret is delicious!"*
18 *But little do they know that the dead are there, that her guests are in the depths of the grave.*

CHAPTER 9

KINGDOM WORK

Proverbs 9:1-18

Key Verse: "Instruct a wise man and he will be wiser still; teach a righteous man and he will add to his learning."

— Proverbs 9:9

According to Pastor Gordon MacDonald,[1] a leader has to deal with four basic types of people. First, there are the VIPs — the very important people. They are today's leaders, and they help the primary leader accomplish his goals. By and large, they are self-sufficient men who require little of the leader other than direction, plus his respect and trust. From them he often receives strength and encouragement, for as the wise man writes, "As iron sharpens iron, so one man sharpens another."[2]

The second group are the VTPs — very trainable people. These are tomorrow's leaders. They are like the VIPs in talent and temperament, but they lack their experience and maturity. In order to achieve their full potential as men of God, they must be trained and discipled. Although their training requires a considerable amount of the leader's time and energy, it is time well spent. By investing himself in them, he multiplies his effectiveness.

The third group are the VNPs — very nice people. They like to be seen with the leader and count him as their friend. Being generous by nature, they make things like their lake house or their condo in the mountains available for the leader's personal use. Their kindness is both a blessing and a burden. Even as it refreshes him, it also tempts him. The VNPs are fun to be with and make few demands, but, by the same token, they seldom make a significant contribution to the accomplishment of the leader's vision.

The fourth group are the VDPs — very draining people. They tend to be insecure persons with a long history of rejection. Because the leader is a compassionate man, they are drawn to him. Once he gives them his attention, they fasten themselves to him, demanding more and more of his life. If he is not careful, their neediness will consume him. While he must be available to them, lest he lose touch with the painful reality of human need, he must also guard himself, lest their neediness consume him.

In my work as a pastor, I find it not only helpful, but necessary to monitor my ministry in order to make sure I am investing myself where it will produce the greatest return for the Kingdom. For me, that means investing in the lives of the VTPs — those men who will be tomorrow's leaders. Without a doubt, my greatest sense of fulfillment comes in seeing them succeed. Through them my efforts are multiplied many times over.

In order to maintain my spiritual vitality, I must then balance my ministry relationships with nourishing friendships. These are reciprocal relationships in which each of us finds food for our soul. We exchange ideas, discuss the Scriptures, joke together, play together and pray together, not as teacher and disciple, but as friend with friend. Spiritual ministry does take place, but it is a consequence of our friendship rather than a goal.

By monitoring both my ministry and my relationships, I am better able to fulfill my leadership responsibilities while maintaining a spiritually and emotionally healthy life. When I fall short of these high ideals, as I often do, God is faithful both to discipline and to restore me.

ACTION STEPS:

☐ How do you see yourself? Are you a primary leader, a VIP, a VTP, a VNP or a VDP? Explain why you think of yourself in that way. Be specific.

☐ Examine the key relationships in your life to see where you are investing yourself. Are your personal investments in the lives of others producing fruit or are you investing inordinate amounts of time for little or no return?

☐ Make a list of the changes you need to make in order for your relationships to become more spiritually productive. Be specific.

THOUGHT FOR THE DAY:

"The trouble with a great many men is that they spread themselves out over too much ground. They fail in everything. If they would only put their life into one channel, and keep it, they would accomplish something. They make no impression, because they do a little work here and a little work there...lay yourselves on the altar of God, and then concentrate on some one work."[3]

— D. L. Moody

PRAYER:

Lord, forgive me for trying to be all things to all people. Help me to live a God-centered life rather than a need-centered one. Fulfill Your purposes in my life. In the name of Jesus I pray. Amen.

PROVERBS 10

1 *The proverbs of Solomon: A wise son brings joy to his father, but a foolish son grief to his mother.*

2 *Ill-gotten treasures are of no value, but righteousness delivers from death.*

3 *The* LORD *does not let the righteous go hungry but he thwarts the craving of the wicked.*

4 *Lazy hands make a man poor, but diligent hands bring wealth.*

5 *He who gathers crops in summer is a wise son, but he who sleeps during harvest is a disgraceful son.*

6 *Blessings crown the head of the righteous, but violence overwhelms the mouth of the wicked.*

7 *The memory of the righteous will be a blessing, but the name of the wicked will rot.*

8 *The wise in heart accept commands, but a chattering fool comes to ruin.*

9 *The man of integrity walks securely, but he who takes crooked paths will be found out.*

10 *He who winks maliciously causes grief, and a chattering fool comes to ruin.*

11 *The mouth of the righteous is a fountain of life, but violence overwhelms the mouth of the wicked.*

12 *Hatred stirs up dissension, but love covers over all wrongs.*

13 *Wisdom is found on the lips of the discerning, but a rod is for the back of him who lacks judgment.*

14 *Wise men store up knowledge, but the mouth of a fool invites ruin.*

15 *The wealth of the rich is their fortified city, but poverty is the ruin of the poor.*

16 *The wages of the righteous bring them life, but the income of the wicked brings them punishment.*

17 *He who heeds discipline shows the way to life, but whoever ignores correction leads others astray.*

18 *He who conceals his hatred has lying lips, and whoever spreads slander is a fool.*

19 *When words are many, sin is not absent, but he who holds his tongue is wise.*

PROVERBS 10

20 *The tongue of the righteous is choice silver, but the heart of the wicked is of little value.*

21 *The lips of the righteous nourish many, but fools die for lack of judgment.*

22 *The blessing of the* LORD *brings wealth, and he adds no trouble to it.*

23 *A fool finds pleasure in evil conduct, but a man of understanding delights in wisdom.*

24 *What the wicked dreads will overtake him; what the righteous desire will be granted.*

25 *When the storm has swept by, the wicked are gone, but the righteous stand firm forever.*

26 *As vinegar to the teeth and smoke to the eyes, so is a sluggard to those who send him.*

27 *The fear of the* LORD *adds length to life, but the years of the wicked are cut short.*

28 *The prospect of the righteous is joy, but the hopes of the wicked come to nothing.*

29 *The way of the* LORD *is a refuge for the righteous, but it is the ruin of those who do evil.*

30 *The righteous will never be uprooted, but the wicked will not remain in the land.*

31 *The mouth of the righteous brings forth wisdom, but a perverse tongue will be cut out.*

32 *The lips of the righteous know what is fitting, but the mouth of the wicked only what is perverse.*

CHAPTER 10

PROPHETIC WORDS

Proverbs 10:1-32

Key verse: "The mouth of the righteous is a fountain of life, but violence overwhelms the mouth of the wicked."

— Proverbs 10:11

Few things in life are more powerful than the spoken word. It can heal or hurt, inspire or intimidate, comfort or crush. "The mouth of the righteous is a fountain of life," declares the wise man, "but violence overwhelms the mouth of the wicked."[1] Again he proclaims, "Reckless words pierce like a sword, but the tongue of the wise brings healing."[2]

As husbands and fathers, our words are especially powerful. This truth was driven home to me in a most painful way some months ago. My wife Brenda and I were sharing on a deeper level than had theretofore been possible, when suddenly she began to sob. Through her tears she related an incident that had taken place nearly thirty years earlier. Although I had long since forgotten it, the mere memory of my words, three decades later, still had the power to make her cry.

Carelessly, I had said some hurtful, manipulative thing, as young men often do, and then had forgotten all about it. For me it was a thing of the past, over and done. But Brenda hadn't forgotten, perhaps she couldn't forget. My reckless words had sorely wounded her. They had shaped the way she saw herself and our relationship, and now thirty years later, she still lived with the pain of their wounding.

Belatedly, I apologized and received her forgiveness, but nothing I did could undo the wounds my reckless words had caused. Like water spilled on the ground which cannot be recovered, my words could not be taken back. With heartfelt sincerity I promised her that with God's help, in the future I would carefully guard the things I said.

Even as a reckless word wounds, so a well-spoken word gives life. It nourishes the soul, encourages the spirit and affirms personal worth.

The words of a parent are especially powerful, even prophetic. What a father believes about his children is important, but it is of limited benefit if he does not express it. When he speaks it, something almost magical happens. His words become a mirror, enabling his children to see themselves as he sees them. Not infrequently the things he sees — the character strengths he affirms, the gifts and talents he identifies, the future possibilities he envisions — give substance to his children's own secret dreams. His words become the first tangible evidence that their dreams are truly possible.

Some years ago, a group of undergraduates at the University of Wisconsin formed an all-male literary club. There were some brilliant young men in the club with real literary talent, and they were determined to bring out the best in each other. At each meeting, one of them would read a story or essay he had written, and the others would critique it. They were merciless. Each manuscript was picked apart, no punches were pulled. To their way of thinking, it was the only way to really develop their talent.

When the coeds heard about the club, they naturally formed one of their own. They too read their manuscripts aloud and offered constructive criticism, but it was criticism of a much gentler nature. Instead of focusing on the weaknesses of each manuscript, they looked for positive things to say. All efforts, however feeble, were encouraged.

The impact of each approach was not fully realized until several years later when an alumnus made an analysis of his classmates' careers. Not one of those bright young men had made a literary reputation of any kind. The coed club, on the other hand, had given rise to half a dozen successful writers, some of national prominence, including Marjorie Kinnan Rawlings, author of *The Yearling*.[3] Coincidence? I think not. The amount of raw talent was much the same in both groups. But while the coeds affirmed one another's talent, the men, with their penchant for merciless criticism, promoted self-doubt.

ACTION STEPS:

☐ Examine your speech. What kind of emotional climate do you create with your words? Do the remarks you make encourage or intimidate your co-workers, your spouse and your children?

☐ Ask your wife and children to list five encouraging things you have said to them in the last seven days. If they cannot remember that many, then make a point of being more affirming.

THOUGHT FOR THE DAY:

"Every man must be persuaded, even if he is in rags, that he is immensely, immensely important. Everyone must respect him and make him respect himself, too....Give him great, great hopes. He needs them, especially if he is young. Spoil him. Yes, make him grow proud."[4]

— Ugo Bette

PRAYER:

Lord, forgive me, for I have sinned with my lips. How I wish I could take back the hurtful things I've said — careless words spoken without thinking, harsh words spoken out of hurt, spiteful words spoken in anger. O Lord, do what I cannot do. Heal the wounds I have caused and restore that which I have destroyed. In the name of Jesus I pray. Amen.

PROVERBS 11

1 *The* LORD *abhors dishonest scales, but accurate weights are his delight.*

2 *When pride comes, then comes disgrace, but with humility comes wisdom.*

3 *The integrity of the upright guides them, but the unfaithful are destroyed by their duplicity.*

4 *Wealth is worthless in the day of wrath, but righteousness delivers from death.*

5 *The righteousness of the blameless makes a straight way for them, but the wicked are brought down by their own wickedness.*

6 *The righteousness of the upright delivers them, but the unfaithful are trapped by evil desires.*

7 *When a wicked man dies, his hope perishes; all he expected from his power comes to nothing.*

8 *The righteous man is rescued from trouble, and it comes on the wicked instead.*

9 *With his mouth the godless destroys his neighbor, but through knowledge the righteous escape.*

10 *When the righteous prosper, the city rejoices; when the wicked perish, there are shouts of joy.*

11 *Through the blessing of the upright a city is exalted, but by the mouth of the wicked it is destroyed.*

12 *A man who lacks judgment derides his neighbor, but a man of understanding holds his tongue.*

13 *A gossip betrays a confidence, but a trustworthy man keeps a secret.*

14 *For lack of guidance a nation falls, but many advisers make victory sure.*

15 *He who puts up security for another will surely suffer, but whoever refuses to strike hands in pledge is safe.*

16 *A kindhearted woman gains respect, but ruthless men gain only wealth.*

17 *A kind man benefits himself, but a cruel man brings trouble on himself.*

PROVERBS 11

18 *The wicked man earns deceptive wages, but he who sows righteousness reaps a sure reward.*

19 *The truly righteous man attains life, but he who pursues evil goes to his death.*

20 *The* LORD *detests men of perverse heart but he delights in those whose ways are blameless.*

21 *Be sure of this: The wicked will not go unpunished, but those who are righteous will go free.*

22 *Like a gold ring in a pig's snout is a beautiful woman who shows no discretion.*

23 *The desire of the righteous ends only in good, but the hope of the wicked only in wrath.*

24 *One man gives freely, yet gains even more; another withholds unduly, but comes to poverty.*

25 *A generous man will prosper; he who refreshes others will himself be refreshed.*

26 *People curse the man who hoards grain, but blessing crowns him who is willing to sell.*

27 *He who seeks good finds goodwill, but evil comes to him who searches for it.*

28 *Whoever trusts in his riches will fall, but the righteous will thrive like a green leaf.*

29 *He who brings trouble on his family will inherit only wind, and the fool will be servant to the wise.*

30 *The fruit of the righteous is a tree of life, and he who wins souls is wise.*

31 *If the righteous receive their due on earth, how much more the ungodly and the sinner!*

CHAPTER 11

HOLY HUGS

Proverbs 11:1-31

Key verses: "One man gives freely, yet gains even more; another withholds unduly, but comes to poverty. A generous man will prosper; he who refreshes others will himself be refreshed."

— Proverbs 11:24,25

As I stepped out of the car, a gust of wind caused the cold to pierce me like a knife. Involuntarily, I tugged up the collar of my overcoat and tried to burrow into its warmth. Thank God I've got a home, I thought. Life on the streets would be deadly in this weather.

"You's gots some wools, man?"

The voice was raspy, harsh sounding, and when I turned to see who had spoken, he began pleading. "I's needs some wools bad. I's freezen in dis col'."

He stood there shivering as I looked him up and down. I guessed him to be about forty, but he looked older. His lips were cracked from the cold, and his skin was chapped and raw. The jacket he was wearing had a broken zipper and was badly worn, especially at the elbows where the lining was showing through. Underneath he wore something resembling a cardigan sweater over a faded flannel shirt.

As I stood there with the north wind tugging at my wool coat, my mind flashed back to the series of events that had brought me to this moment. For days God had been dealing with me about the plight of the homeless. It seemed that every time I turned on the television, there was another special about some family living under a bridge or in their car. As Christmas drew near, and an unexpected cold spell plunged temperatures near zero, I felt more and more compelled to do something, but what?

Each time I prayed, God seemed to remind me of a double-breasted, navy blue overcoat hanging in my closet. It was nearly ten years old, but looked hardly worn. For warmth and durability, it was the best coat I had ever owned. A couple of years earlier I had replaced it with a newer style, but I couldn't bear to part with it, so I kept it hanging in the downstairs coat closet. Now it was a sore point between the Lord and me. I sensed that He wanted me to give it to some homeless person, but I couldn't bring myself to part with it.

During my devotional time that morning God spoke to me so clearly that I knew I could resist no longer. After telling my secretary that I was leaving, I drove home to collect the coat and a matching wool scarf. When Brenda asked me how I would know who to give it to, I answered, "God will show me; and if He doesn't, I will just give it to Mother Tucker's rescue mission."

That's where I was now — in front of Mother Tucker's — being harassed by this...this homeless wino. In disgust I turned my back on him and opened the rear door of my car. When he saw me take the coat out of the car, his eyes lit up with desire. "I's needs some wools, man..." he began as I ignored him and started walking toward the front door of the mission. He followed me, pleading, and as I started to open the door, it hit me. He was the answer to my prayer, the man to whom God wanted me to give my coat.

I turned so swiftly that I almost bumped into him. Thrusting the coat at him, I said, "Here try this on."

In an instant he had the coat on and buttoned up. It fit perfectly, as I knew it would. Stepping closer, I put the matching wool scarf around his neck and tucked it inside the front of his coat. Before I could step back, he wrapped his arms around me and pulled me to his chest in a bear hug. He smelled like booze and body odor and damp clothes, but I didn't mind. His was the holiest hug I've ever received. In that moment it was as if God Himself were hugging me.

ACTION STEPS:

☐ In prayer, ask God to give you a compassionate heart for all those less fortunate than you.

☐ Is there anyone in your immediate circle of friends and associates who is in need? A single parent perhaps who cannot afford to send her son to church camp? A newlywed couple who need some help repairing their car? If you can't think of anyone, ask your pastor. He is probably aware of some desperate need within the church family.

☐ In prayer ask God what He would have you do to meet these needs. Be sensitive to the thoughts and impressions that come to you as you wait quietly before Him. That's usually how He speaks. Now go and do as He directs you.

THOUGHT FOR THE DAY:

"Going to town one day to sell some small articles, Abba Agathon met a cripple on the roadside, paralysed in his legs, who asked him where he was going. Abba Agathon replied, 'To town, to sell some things.' The other said, 'Do me the favor of carrying me there.' So he carried him to the town. The cripple said to him, 'Put me down where you sell your wares.' He did so. When he had sold an article, the cripple asked, 'What did you sell it for?' and he told him the price. The other said, 'Buy me a cake,' and he bought it. When Abba Agathon had sold all his wares, the cripple wanted to go, and he said to him, 'Are you going back?' and he replied, 'Yes.' Then he said, 'Do me the favor of carrying me back to the place where you found me.' Once more picking him up, he carried him back to that place. Then the cripple said, 'Agathon, you are filled with divine blessings, in heaven and on earth.' Raising his eyes, Agathon saw no man; it was an angel of the Lord, come to try him."[1]

— The Desert Christian

PRAYER:

Lord, thank You for letting me know the joy of sharing with those less fortunate than I. Forgive me for the times I am blind or insensitive to their needs. Don't give up on me. Surely I will one day be the man You have called me to be. In the name of Jesus I pray. Amen.

PROVERBS 12

1 *Whoever loves discipline loves knowledge, but he who hates correction is stupid.*

2 *A good man obtains favor from the* LORD, *but the* LORD *condemns a crafty man.*

3 *A man cannot be established through wickedness, but the righteous cannot be uprooted.*

4 *A wife of noble character is her husband's crown, but a disgraceful wife is like decay in his bones.*

5 *The plans of the righteous are just, but the advice of the wicked is deceitful.*

6 *The words of the wicked lie in wait for blood, but the speech of the upright rescues them.*

7 *Wicked men are overthrown and are no more, but the house of the righteous stands firm.*

8 *A man is praised according to his wisdom, but men with warped minds are despised.*

9 *Better to be a nobody and yet have a servant than pretend to be somebody and have no food.*

10 *A righteous man cares for the needs of his animal, but the kindest acts of the wicked are cruel.*

11 *He who works his land will have abundant food, but he who chases fantasies lacks judgment.*

12 *The wicked desire the plunder of evil men, but the root of the righteous flourishes.*

13 *An evil man is trapped by his sinful talk, but a righteous man escapes trouble.*

14 *From the fruit of his lips a man is filled with good things as surely as the work of his hands rewards him.*

15 *The way of a fool seems right to him, but a wise man listens to advice.*

16 *A fool shows his annoyance at once, but a prudent man overlooks an insult.*

17 *A truthful witness gives honest testimony, but a false witness tells lies.*

PROVERBS 12

18 *Reckless words pierce like a sword, but the tongue of the wise brings healing.*

19 *Truthful lips endure forever, but a lying tongue lasts only a moment.*

20 *There is deceit in the hearts of those who plot evil, but joy for those who promote peace.*

21 *No harm befalls the righteous, but the wicked have their fill of trouble.*

22 *The* LORD *detests lying lips, but he delights in men who are truthful.*

23 *A prudent man keeps his knowledge to himself, but the heart of fools blurts out folly.*

24 *Diligent hands will rule, but laziness ends in slave labor.*

25 *An anxious heart weighs a man down, but a kind word cheers him up.*

26 *A righteous man is cautious in friendship, but the way of the wicked leads them astray.*

27 *The lazy man does not roast his game, but the diligent man prizes his possessions.*

28 *In the way of righteousness there is life; along that path is immortality.*

CHAPTER 12

RECKLESS WORDS

Proverbs 12:1-28

Key verse: "Reckless words pierce like a sword, but the tongue of the wise brings healing."

— Proverbs 12:18

Let me tell you a story, a true story. It's not my story, it's Dick Gregory's. But in another sense, it is mine, and it is yours too, for who among us hasn't been sorely wounded by a careless remark or a cruel comment?

"It was on a Thursday, the day before the Negro payday. The eagle always flew on Friday. The teacher was asking each student how much his father would give to the Community Chest. On Friday night, each kid would get the money from his father, and on Monday he would bring it to the school. I decided I was going to buy me a Daddy right then. I had money in my pocket from shining shoes and selling papers, and whatever Helene Tucker pledged for her Daddy I was going to top it. And I'd hand the money right in. I wasn't going to wait until Monday to buy me a Daddy.

"I was shaking, scared to death. The teacher opened her book and started calling out names alphabetically.

"'Helene Tucker?'

"'My Daddy said he'd give two dollars and fifty cents.'

"That made me feel pretty good. It wouldn't take too much to top that. I had almost three dollars in dimes and quarters in my pocket. I stuck my hand in my pocket and held onto the money, waiting for her to call my name. But the teacher closed her book after she called everybody else in the class.

"I stood up and raised my hand.

"'What is it now?'

"'You forgot me.'

"She turned toward the blackboard. 'I don't have time to be playing with you, Richard.'

"'My Daddy said he'd....'

"'Sit down, Richard, you're disturbing the class.'

"'My Daddy said he'd give...fifteen dollars.'

"She turned around and looked mad. 'We are collecting this money for you and your kind, Richard Gregory. If your Daddy can give fifteen dollars you have no business being on relief.'

"'I got it right now, I got it right now, my Daddy gave it to me to turn in today, my Daddy said....'

"'And furthermore,' she said, looking right at me, her nostrils getting big and her lips getting thin and her eyes opening wide, 'we know you don't have a Daddy.'

"Helene Tucker turned around, her eyes full of tears. She felt sorry for me. Then I couldn't see her too well because I was crying, too.

"'Sit down, Richard.'

"And I always thought the teacher kind of liked me. She always picked me to wash the blackboard on Friday, after school. That was a big thrill, it made me feel important. If I didn't wash it, come Monday the school might not function right.

"'Where are you going, Richard?'

"I walked out of school that day, and for a long time I didn't go back very often. There was shame there."[1]

Perhaps his teacher was being cruel, but more likely she was just insensitive, unaware of how desperately Dick needed to feel a part of the class. Whatever the reason, the damage was done. Her reckless words shamed Dick, and it was a long time before he got over his humiliation.

Maybe as you read that story you found yourself reliving some sorrowful memory of your own. With painful clarity the hurtful words returned, and with them the old feelings of shame and rejection. Once more you find yourself raging on the inside, but still powerless to do anything about it. Let me encourage you to surrender your feelings to the Lord and make peace with your pain. Invite Him to redeem your hurt, to use it to make you compassionate and sensitive to the sufferings of others. Do this, and what was intended for your destruction will become material for ministry.

ACTION STEPS:

☐ What did you feel as you read this story? Shame? Anger? Hurt? Compassion? Such is the wounding power of reckless words. Think about that for a moment and then ask the Lord to set a watch over your lips, lest you wound someone with your words.

☐ Perhaps you now remember something hurtful that you said, someone who was sorely wounded by your words. Telephone that person or write a letter seeking his forgiveness. Now pray and ask God to heal the wounds you caused.

THOUGHT FOR THE DAY:

"Life in a way is like those electric bump cars at the amusement park. We just run at each other and smile and bump and away we go.

"How are you doing —
bump, bump,
Hi, Motormouth —
bump, bump,
Great, fantastic —
bump, bump, bump,
And somebody slips out and dies because there is no one to talk to.
bump, bump, bump."[2]

— Bob Benson

PRAYER:

Lord, I pray for all the "Dick Gregorys" of the world, including me. We have been wounded, ridiculed and rejected by those we trusted. Bitterness tempts us, as do self-doubt and pity. Heal our brokenness, O Lord. Restore our innocence and our faith. In the name of Jesus I pray. Amen.

PROVERBS 13

1 *A wise son heeds his father's instruction, but a mocker does not listen to rebuke.*

2 *From the fruit of his lips a man enjoys good things, but the unfaithful have a craving for violence.*

3 *He who guards his lips guards his life, but he who speaks rashly will come to ruin.*

4 *The sluggard craves and gets nothing, but the desires of the diligent are fully satisfied.*

5 *The righteous hate what is false, but the wicked bring shame and disgrace.*

6 *Righteousness guards the man of integrity, but wickedness overthrows the sinner.*

7 *One man pretends to be rich, yet has nothing; another pretends to be poor, yet has great wealth.*

8 *A man's riches may ransom his life, but a poor man hears no threat.*

9 *The light of the righteous shines brightly, but the lamp of the wicked is snuffed out.*

10 *Pride only breeds quarrels, but wisdom is found in those who take advice.*

11 *Dishonest money dwindles away, but he who gathers money little by little makes it grow.*

12 *Hope deferred makes the heart sick, but a longing fulfilled is a tree of life.*

13 *He who scorns instruction will pay for it, but he who respects a command is rewarded.*

14 *The teaching of the wise is a fountain of life, turning a man from the snares of death.*

15 *Good understanding wins favor, but the way of the unfaithful is hard.*

16 *Every prudent man acts out of knowledge, but a fool exposes his folly.*

17 *A wicked messenger falls into trouble, but a trustworthy envoy brings healing.*

PROVERBS 13

18 *He who ignores discipline comes to poverty and shame, but whoever heeds correction is honored.*

19 *A longing fulfilled is sweet to the soul, but fools detest turning from evil.*

20 *He who walks with the wise grows wise, but a companion of fools suffers harm.*

21 *Misfortune pursues the sinner, but prosperity is the reward of the righteous.*

22 *A good man leaves an inheritance for his children's children, but a sinner's wealth is stored up for the righteous.*

23 *A poor man's field may produce abundant food, but injustice sweeps it away.*

24 *He who spares the rod hates his son, but he who loves him is careful to discipline him.*

25 *The righteous eat to their hearts' content, but the stomach of the wicked goes hungry.*

CHAPTER 13

MONEY MATTERS

Proverbs 13:1-25

Key verse: "Dishonest money dwindles away, but he who gathers money little by little makes it grow."

— Proverbs 13:11

Larry had two good friends. One was named Walter and the other Norman. They were unlike each other in every way except for their faith in Jesus Christ. Even in their faith they were decidedly different. Walter was actively involved in all the activities of his church; he was highly visible and much loved by everyone. Norman, on the other hand, only attended church on Sunday morning and maintained a low profile. They were both, however, extraordinarily generous givers.

In the course of time their careers went in opposite directions. Walter made a considerable amount of money in a relatively short time and seemed on the verge of becoming a wealthy man. Unfortunately, things did not work out, and he eventually lost everything. Norman, according to those who knew him best, seemed to have the proverbial Midas touch — everything he touched turned to gold. He simply went from success to success.

Only God knows for sure why Walter failed in business while Norman prospered, but those who know them both make some interesting observations. Most obvious is the way they each view money. According to their mutual friend Larry, Walter saw making money as the ultimate goal in business, while Norman considered it merely a consequence — important to be sure, but not the only reason for being in business.

There were other differences too. For instance, Norman limited his involvement to ventures for which he was trained. Even then he was careful to investigate each opportunity fully to make sure there were no surprises. Once he became involved, he developed a detailed plan and followed it through to completion.

Walter, on the other hand, was willing to do business with almost anyone as long as the enterprise was not immoral or illegal. He loved to wheel and deal. The higher the stakes and the greater the risks, the better he liked it. Not infrequently, his deals involved a certain amount of intrigue, and although he was an honest man, the same could not always be said for his partners.

Despite the fact that he was an intelligent man, the excitement of the deal seemed to have a way of blinding him to the risks involved. While he acknowledged their existence, in an academic sort of way, he never really comprehended them on an emotional level. They simply were not real to him. As far as he was concerned, every deal was a "sure thing." This trait made him a tremendous promoter, and he had an amazing ability to raise venture capital. Unfortunately, it also made him a poor businessman. When he lost his shirt, as it were, a lot of trusting people lost theirs as well.

What is the point in telling you all of this? Just this: success in business is often nothing more than knowing and heeding the principles of Holy Scripture. Although the Bible is not a textbook on financial matters, it does have a considerable amount to say on the subject. He who manages his business or his personal affairs accordingly will prosper, and he who ignores these biblical teachings does so to his own harm.

Some of the more fundamental scriptural principles include:

1) A warning against seeking wealth. "People who want to get rich," according to the apostle Paul, "fall into temptation and a trap and into many foolish and harmful desires that plunge men into ruin and destruction."[1]

2) A warning against greed. Jesus said, "...'Watch out! Be on your guard against all kinds of greed....'"[2] Studies show that most bad investments are made out of greed. A man sees an opportunity to get rich quick, and it blinds him to the risks involved. Inevitably, his family suffers the consequences. As the ancient sage observed, "A greedy man brings trouble to his family...."[3]

3) **A warning against chasing fantasies.** The writer of Proverbs declares: "He who works his land will have abundant food, but he who chases fantasies lacks judgment."[4]

4) **An exhortation to exercise good judgment and seek wise counsel.** If something seems too good to be true, it probably is: "A simple man believes anything, but a prudent man gives thought to his steps."[5] "He who walks with the wise grows wise, but a companion of fools suffers harm."[6]

5) **An exhortation to be diligent in everything.** "The plans of the diligent lead to profit as surely as haste leads to poverty."[7]

It is a wise man who makes himself knowledgeable in these matters.

ACTION STEPS:

☐ Examine your personal and/or business practices. Based on your findings, make a list of the principles by which you operate.

☐ List the five biblical principles for financial management and carry it with you in your wallet or daytimer. Memorize the accompanying Scriptures.

☐ Examine your personal and/or business practices in light of these principles. What adjustments, if any, do you need to make? Be specific.

THOUGHT FOR THE DAY:

"Be careful who you associate with lest you become entangled with their excesses and be brought down with them.

"Choose character above riches and truthfulness above prosperity."[8]

— A Private Journal

PRAYER:

Lord, help me to be content without being complacent, to be industrious without being greedy, to be prudent without being obsessively cautious. Above all else, give me a thankful heart. In the name of Jesus I pray. Amen.

PROVERBS 14

1 *The wise woman builds her house, but with her own hands the foolish one tears hers down.*

2 *He whose walk is upright fears the* LORD, *but he whose ways are devious despises him.*

3 *A fool's talk brings a rod to his back, but the lips of the wise protect them.*

4 *Where there are no oxen, the manger is empty, but from the strength of an ox comes an abundant harvest.*

5 *A truthful witness does not deceive, but a false witness pours out lies.*

6 *The mocker seeks wisdom and finds none, but knowledge comes easily to the discerning.*

7 *Stay away from a foolish man, for you will not find knowledge on his lips.*

8 *The wisdom of the prudent is to give thought to their ways, but the folly of fools is deception.*

9 *Fools mock at making amends for sin, but goodwill is found among the upright.*

10 *Each heart knows its own bitterness, and no one else can share its joy.*

11 *The house of the wicked will be destroyed, but the tent of the upright will flourish.*

12 *There is a way that seems right to a man, but in the end it leads to death.*

13 *Even in laughter the heart may ache, and joy may end in grief.*

14 *The faithless will be fully repaid for their ways, and the good man rewarded for his.*

15 *A simple man believes anything, but a prudent man gives thought to his steps.*

16 *A wise man fears the* LORD *and shuns evil, but a fool is hotheaded and reckless.*

17 *A quick-tempered man does foolish things, and a crafty man is hated.*

18 *The simple inherit folly, but the prudent are crowned with knowledge.*

PROVERBS 14

19 *Evil men will bow down in the presence of the good, and the wicked at the gates of the righteous.*

20 *The poor are shunned even by their neighbors, but the rich have many friends.*

21 *He who despises his neighbor sins, but blessed is he who is kind to the needy.*

22 *Do not those who plot evil go astray? But those who plan what is good find love and faithfulness.*

23 *All hard work brings a profit, but mere talk leads only to poverty.*

24 *The wealth of the wise is their crown, but the folly of fools yields folly.*

25 *A truthful witness saves lives, but a false witness is deceitful.*

26 *He who fears the* LORD *has a secure fortress, and for his children it will be a refuge.*

27 *The fear of the* LORD *is a fountain of life, turning a man from the snares of death.*

28 *A large population is a king's glory, but without subjects a prince is ruined.*

29 *A patient man has great understanding, but a quick-tempered man displays folly.*

30 *A heart at peace gives life to the body, but envy rots the bones.*

31 *He who oppresses the poor shows contempt for their Maker, but whoever is kind to the needy honors God.*

32 *When calamity comes, the wicked are brought down, but even in death the righteous have a refuge.*

33 *Wisdom reposes in the heart of the discerning and even among fools she lets herself be known.*

34 *Righteousness exalts a nation, but sin is a disgrace to any people.*

35 *A king delights in a wise servant, but a shameful servant incurs his wrath.*

CHAPTER 14

A National Disgrace

Proverbs 14:1-35

Key verse: "Righteousness exalts a nation, but sin is a disgrace to any people."

— Proverbs 14:34

What's happening in America is a national disgrace. "The 1992 report of the National Research Council says the United States is now the most violent of all industrialized nations. For example, the U.S. homicide rate for 15- to 24-year-old males is 7 times higher than Canada's and 40 times higher than Japan's. The U.S. has one of the highest teenage pregnancy rates, the highest teen abortion rate, and the highest level of drug use among young people in the developed world. Youth suicide has tripled in the past 25 years, and a survey of more than 2,000 Rhode Island students, grades six through nine, found that two out of three boys and one of two girls thought it 'acceptable for a man to force sex on a woman' if they had been dating for six months or more."[1]

Like many of us, criminologist James Q. Wilson wanted to know where the United States had gone wrong, so he set out to research the history of crime in America. In the process he stumbled on a historical fact he had not noticed before. The decrease in crime in the nineteenth century followed a widespread religious revival known as the Second Great Awakening. Repentance and renewal spread across the country, bringing moral reform. Once more American society came to respect the values of sobriety, hard work, self-restraint — what sociologists call the Protestant ethic.[2]

Then came the twentieth century, and by the 1920s and 1930s a host of new ideas were challenging the prevailing moral and religious values. Darwin's theory of evolution led people to see all things, including morality, as being in flux. The philosophy of logical positivism asserted a radical distinction between facts (which could be scientifically proven) and values (which positivism held were mere expressions of feeling, not objective truth), causing many people to conclude that morality was relative and personal. As a result, by the 1960s, America was experiencing a crisis of moral authority, eroded belief in objective moral norms, the sexual revolution and a spiraling crime rate.

As Chuck Colson so succinctly puts it, "The lesson of history is clear: When Christian belief is strong, the crime rate falls; when Christian belief weakens, the crime rate climbs. Widespread religious belief creates a shared social ethic that acts as a restraint on the dark side of human nature."[3]

This is not a new thought. It was first expressed by the author of Proverbs thousands of years ago: "Righteousness exalts a nation, but sin is a disgrace to any people."[4]

Two hundred years ago John Adams said, "Our constitution was made only for a moral and religious people. It is wholly inadequate for the government of any other."[5]

And historians Will and Ariel Durant, after studying two thousand years of Western civilization, concluded, "There is no significant example in history...of a society successfully maintaining moral life without the aid of religion."[6]

Congress can pass a massive anti-crime bill if it chooses. New tax dollars can put thousands more law enforcement officers on the streets. Judges can hand down harsh sentences for repeat offenders, and hundreds of new prisons can be built to handle all the criminals, but if America does not return to her moral and spiritual roots, it will all be in vain.

ACTION STEPS:

☐ Familiarize yourself with organizations like Focus on the Family's Citizen's Council and the Christian Coalition. Pray about becoming actively involved.

☐ Familiarize yourself with the spiritual truths of American history by reading books like *The Light and the Glory* by Peter Marshall and David Manuel (Fleming H. Revell) and *America's God and Country Encyclopedia of Quotations* compiled by William J. Federer (Fame). To become informed on current issues read *A Dance With Deception* by Charles Colson (Word).

☐ Organize a men's prayer group to pray for our nation. (See 2 Chronicles 7:14.)

THOUGHT FOR THE DAY:

"It was not until I went into the churches of America and heard her pulpits flame with righteousness that I understood her greatness... Religion is indispensable to the maintenance of republican institutions...."

— Alexis de Tocqueville

PRAYER:

"...'O Lord, the great and awesome God, who keeps His covenant of love with all who love Him and obey His commands, we have sinned and done wrong. We have been wicked and have rebelled; we have turned away from Your commands and laws...Now, our God, hear the prayers and petitions of Your servant...We do not make requests of You because we are righteous, but because of Your great mercy. O Lord, listen! O Lord, forgive! O Lord, hear and act! For Your sake, O my God, do not delay...."[7]

PROVERBS 15

1 *A gentle answer turns away wrath, but a harsh word stirs up anger.*

2 *The tongue of the wise commends knowledge, but the mouth of the fool gushes folly.*

3 *The eyes of the* LORD *are everywhere, keeping watch on the wicked and the good.*

4 *The tongue that brings healing is a tree of life, but a deceitful tongue crushes the spirit.*

5 *A fool spurns his father's discipline, but whoever heeds correction shows prudence.*

6 *The house of the righteous contains great treasure, but the income of the wicked brings them trouble.*

7 *The lips of the wise spread knowledge; not so the hearts of fools.*

8 *The* LORD *detests the sacrifice of the wicked, but the prayer of the upright pleases him.*

9 *The* LORD *detests the way of the wicked but he loves those who pursue righteousness.*

10 *Stern discipline awaits him who leaves the path; he who hates correction will die.*

11 *Death and Destruction lie open before the* LORD *— how much more the hearts of men!*

12 *A mocker resents correction; he will not consult the wise.*

13 *A happy heart makes the face cheerful, but heartache crushes the spirit.*

14 *The discerning heart seeks knowledge, but the mouth of a fool feeds on folly.*

15 *All the days of the oppressed are wretched, but the cheerful heart has a continual feast.*

16 *Better a little with the fear of the* LORD *than great wealth with turmoil.*

17 *Better a meal of vegetables where there is love than a fattened calf with hatred.*

18 *A hot-tempered man stirs up dissension, but a patient man calms a quarrel.*

19 *The way of the sluggard is blocked with thorns, but the path of the upright is a highway.*

PROVERBS 15

20 *A wise son brings joy to his father, but a foolish man despises his mother.*

21 *Folly delights a man who lacks judgment, but a man of understanding keeps a straight course.*

22 *Plans fail for lack of counsel, but with many advisers they succeed.*

23 *A man finds joy in giving an apt reply— and how good is a timely word!*

24 *The path of life leads upward for the wise to keep him from going down to the grave.*

25 *The* LORD *tears down the proud man's house but he keeps the widow's boundaries intact.*

26 *The* LORD *detests the thoughts of the wicked, but those of the pure are pleasing to him.*

27 *A greedy man brings trouble to his family, but he who hates bribes will live.*

28 *The heart of the righteous weighs its answers, but the mouth of the wicked gushes evil.*

29 *The* LORD *is far from the wicked but he hears the prayer of the righteous.*

30 *A cheerful look brings joy to the heart, and good news gives health to the bones.*

31 *He who listens to a life-giving rebuke will be at home among the wise.*

32 *He who ignores discipline despises himself, but whoever heeds correction gains understanding.*

33 *The fear of the* LORD *teaches a man wisdom, and humility comes before honor.*

CHAPTER 15

CONSTRUCTIVE CRITICISM

Proverbs 15:1-33

Key verses: "He who listens to a life-giving rebuke will be at home among the wise. He who ignores discipline despises himself, but whoever heeds correction gains understanding."

— Proverbs 15:31,32

Criticism always makes me feel defensive. I handle it better now, but as a young pastor I often became angry and argumentative when criticized. Stubbornly I defended myself, even when I knew I was wrong. Usually, after I had had time to calm down I would come around, but by then it was often too late. Not infrequently, my angry words wounded a fellow believer, and as the wise man notes, "An offended brother is more unyielding than a fortified city...."[1]

Experience taught me to be more discreet. Although I continued to feel attacked, I learned to watch my words. Unfortunately, I could not hide my defensiveness. (Brenda says I am like the octopus who secretes a black, ink-like liquid when it senses danger. Even though I speak softly, and with great politeness, I emit powerful vibes.)

Regardless of what anyone says to the contrary I continue to find criticism painful. Perhaps that's why it's so hard for me to deal with it. When it is ungrounded, I feel misunderstood and unfairly judged. If it is legitimate, I am grieved because I have not measured up to my own expectations, let alone the expectations of others.

Well do I remember the afternoon two members of the official board of our church met with me to deliver some constructive criticism. They were kind, they did not attack me, but they were also firm in expressing their concerns. As they spoke, I experienced an unbearable sadness. My throat got tight, my eyes teared up and it was all I could do to keep from breaking down. Their concerns were legitimate, the things they were saying were clearly accurate, and I felt like a failure. I'm sure they did not consider me a failure, but in my heart that's how I felt. Although I know I am not the perfect pastor, it always pains me to learn that my shortcomings are obvious to others as well.

We talked at length that afternoon. I sought their advice on ways to address the areas of their concern. After praying together with me, they assured me of their support and once again made themselves available to help in any way they could. All in all it was the most constructive criticism a man could ever hope to receive; still, it was terribly painful.

The Scriptures clearly teach that constructive criticism, painful though it may be, is essential for correction. They declare, "He who ignores discipline despises himself, but whoever heeds correction gains understanding."[2] With that thought in mind, let me share some of the guidelines I find helpful in evaluating and processing criticism.

1) Make it a matter of prayer. There is often an element of truth in even the most malicious criticism. In prayer, ask God if there is anything He is trying to tell you through this criticism. Ask Him to purify your spirit and to ever remind you that He loves the one who may have unjustly criticized you just as much as He loves you.

2) Consider the source. Although God can use anyone to correct us, He generally speaks through trustworthy people. Therefore, I give considerable more weight to criticism when it comes from a peer or a mature believer.

3) Carefully weigh the criticism, separating that which is valid from that which is not. Even the most sincere person is capable of interjecting his personal feelings into a situation; therefore, I am careful not to accept everything at face value. On occasion I have found it beneficial to discuss the criticism with a third person in order to get a more objective view.

4) With God's help make the corrections that are required. It is seldom easy to admit that we are wrong, especially if it means reversing a decision or changing a public policy, but it is absolutely mandatory. "He who heeds discipline shows the way to life, but whoever ignores correction leads others astray."[3]

ACTION STEPS:

☐ Recall the last time you were criticized. How did you respond? Be specific.

☐ Using the four guidelines listed above, reevaluate that criticism. List any insights or conclusions you may have reached. What action, if any, are you planning to take?

THOUGHT FOR THE DAY:

"Indeed, this need of individuals to be right is so great that they are willing to sacrifice themselves, their relationships, and even love for it. This need to be right is also one which produces hostility and cruelty, and causes people to say things that shut them off from communication with both God and man."[4]

— Ruel Howe

PRAYER:

Lord, my need to be right makes it hard for me to accept criticism. I become defensive, justify my behavior or even find fault with the one who seeks to correct me. Forgive me and change me, I pray. Give me a teachable spirit and a humble heart. In the name of Jesus I pray. Amen.

PROVERBS 16

1 *To man belong the plans of the heart, but from the* LORD *comes the reply of the tongue.*

2 *All a man's ways seem innocent to him, but motives are weighed by the* LORD.

3 *Commit to the* LORD *whatever you do, and your plans will succeed.*

4 *The* LORD *works out everything for his own ends — even the wicked for a day of disaster.*

5 *The* LORD *detests all the proud of heart. Be sure of this: They will not go unpunished.*

6 *Through love and faithfulness sin is atoned for; through the fear of the* LORD *a man avoids evil.*

7 *When a man's ways are pleasing to the* LORD, *he makes even his enemies live at peace with him.*

8 *Better a little with righteousness than much gain with injustice.*

9 *In his heart a man plans his course, but the* LORD *determines his steps.*

10 *The lips of a king speak as an oracle, and his mouth should not betray justice.*

11 *Honest scales and balances are from the* LORD; *all the weights in the bag are of his making.*

12 *Kings detest wrongdoing, for a throne is established through righteousness.*

13 *Kings take pleasure in honest lips; they value a man who speaks the truth.*

14 *A king's wrath is a messenger of death, but a wise man will appease it.*

15 *When a king's face brightens, it means life; his favor is like a rain cloud in spring.*

16 *How much better to get wisdom than gold, to choose understanding rather than silver!*

17 *The highway of the upright avoids evil; he who guards his way guards his life.*

18 *Pride goes before destruction, a haughty spirit before a fall.*

PROVERBS 16

19 *Better to be lowly in spirit and among the oppressed than to share plunder with the proud.*

20 *Whoever gives heed to instruction prospers, and blessed is he who trusts in the* LORD.

21 *The wise in heart are called discerning, and pleasant words promote instruction.*

22 *Understanding is a fountain of life to those who have it, but folly brings punishment to fools.*

23 *A wise man's heart guides his mouth, and his lips promote instruction.*

24 *Pleasant words are a honeycomb, sweet to the soul and healing to the bones.*

25 *There is a way that seems right to a man, but in the end it leads to death.*

26 *The laborer's appetite works for him; his hunger drives him on.*

27 *A scoundrel plots evil, and his speech is like a scorching fire.*

28 *A perverse man stirs up dissension, and a gossip separates close friends.*

29 *A violent man entices his neighbor and leads him down a path that is not good.*

30 *He who winks with his eye is plotting perversity; he who purses his lips is bent on evil.*

31 *Gray hair is a crown of splendor; it is attained by a righteous life.*

32 *Better a patient man than a warrior, a man who controls his temper than one who takes a city.*

33 *The lot is cast into the lap, but its every decision is from the* LORD.

CHAPTER 16

THE MUD OR THE STARS?

Proverbs 16:1-33

Key verse: "Pleasant words are a honeycomb, sweet to the soul and healing to the bones."

— Proverbs 16:24

As my ten-year-old daughter hurried toward the car I could tell that something was wrong, and when she slid onto the front seat beside me she burst into tears. Looking at her sitting there with tears running down her cheeks, I thought my heart would break. I wanted to take her in my arms and shield her from the world. I wanted to protect her from all the pain and cruelty that we human beings heap on each other, but I knew I couldn't. Instead, I held her hand and listened as she poured out her anger and humiliation.

When she had finally exhausted her tearful rage, I suggested that we go somewhere and have a hamburger. She agreed, and in a matter of minutes we were seated in a corner booth munching on some fries. While we ate, I told her a story: During World War II a young lady named Thelma Thompson and her soldier husband were stationed at an Army training camp near the Mojave Desert in California. According to Thelma she went to live there to be near her spouse.

"I hated the place," she says. "I loathed it. I had never before been so miserable. My husband was ordered out on maneuvers in the Mojave Desert, and I was left in a tiny shack alone. The heat was unbearable — 125 degrees in the shade of a cactus. Not a soul to talk to but Mexicans and Indians, and they couldn't speak English. The wind blew incessantly, and all the food I ate, and the very air I breathed, were filled with sand, sand, sand!

"I was so utterly wretched, so sorry for myself, that I wrote to my parents. I told them I was giving up and coming home. I said I couldn't stand it one minute longer. I would rather be in jail! My father answered my letter with just two lines — two lines that will always sing in my memory — two lines that completely altered my life:

'Two men looked out from prison bars,
One saw the mud, the other saw the stars.'

"I read those two lines over and over. I was ashamed of myself. I made up my mind I would look for the stars. I made friends with the natives, and their reaction amazed me. When I showed interest in their weaving and pottery, they gave me presents of their favorite pieces which they had refused to show to the tourists. I studied the fascinating forms of the cactus and the yuccas and the Joshua trees. I learned about prairie dogs, watched for the desert sunsets, and hunted for seashells that had been left there millions of years ago when the sands of the desert had been an ocean floor.

"What brought about this astonishing change in me? The Mojave Desert hadn't changed. The Indians hadn't changed. But I had. I had changed my attitude of mind. And by doing so, I transformed a wretched experience into the most exciting adventure of my life. I was stimulated and excited by this new world that I had discovered. I was so excited I wrote a book about it — a novel that was published under the title *Bright Ramparts*. I had looked out of my self-created prison and found the stars."[1]

"Leah," I said, reaching for her hands, "You won't always have the power to change the circumstances in which you find yourself, but you always have the power to choose your attitude. So what's it going to be, girl, are you going to look at the mud or the stars?"

From that day forward those two lines became a motto in our family. Whenever some childhood disappointment or adolescent difficulty tempted Leah to depression, I simply asked, "What are you looking at, sweetheart, the mud or the stars?" The choice wasn't always easy, but inevitably her chin would come up and with a look of fierce determination she would say, "I choose to look at the stars!"

One Sunday evening, when Leah was maybe thirteen or fourteen, I was complaining to Brenda as we drove toward the church. The particulars of that conversation have long since been forgotten, but I do recall that I was putting on quite a show. Suddenly, from the back seat, I heard this adolescent voice:

"'Two men looked out from prison bars,

One saw the mud, the other saw the stars.'

What are you looking at, Dad, the mud or the stars?"

Now, I don't mind telling you that, in spite of being soundly rebuked, that was an unforgettable moment for me. Indeed, it would have been for any father. For a man never knows a prouder moment than when he hears the spiritual values he has endeavored to impress upon his children repeated back to him. In that moment I understood a little more of what Solomon meant when he wrote: "Pleasant words are a honeycomb, sweet to the soul and healing to the bones."[2]

ACTION STEPS:

☐ Take a few minutes and reminiscence. Can you recall a time when one of your parents spoke healing, even life-changing, words to you? If your parents are still living, why not write them a note and thank them.

☐ As a husband and a father, your words have tremendous power for your wife and children. Determine right now that you will speak words of life and not death, that you will affirm and encourage your family at every opportunity.

☐ Memorize Psalm 141:3: "Set a guard over my mouth, O Lord; keep watch over the door of my lips." Make that your daily prayer.

THOUGHT FOR THE DAY:

"Benjamin West, a British artist, tells how he first became aware of his artistic skills. One day his mother went out, leaving him in charge of his little sister Sally. In his mother's absence, he discovered some bottles of colored ink and to amuse her, he began to paint Sally's portrait. In doing so, he made quite a mess of things...spilled numerous ink splotches here and there. When his mother returned, she saw the mess, but said nothing about it. She deliberately looked beyond all that as she picked up the piece of paper. Smiling, she exclaimed, 'Why, it's Sally!' She then stooped and kissed her son. From that time on, Benjamin West would say, 'My mother's kiss made me a painter.'"[3]

— William Barclay

PRAYER:

Lord, I have to confess that more often than not I have eyes only for the mess. In sorrow I have to wonder how many nascent dreams I have crushed with a careless word. Forgive me, Lord, and set a guard over my mouth and a watch over the door of my lips. In the name of Jesus I pray. Amen.

PROVERBS 17

1 *Better a dry crust with peace and quiet than a house full of feasting, with strife.*

2 *A wise servant will rule over a disgraceful son, and will share the inheritance as one of the brothers.*

3 *The crucible for silver and the furnace for gold, but the* LORD *tests the heart.*

4 *A wicked man listens to evil lips; a liar pays attention to a malicious tongue.*

5 *He who mocks the poor shows contempt for their Maker; whoever gloats over disaster will not go unpunished.*

6 *Children's children are a crown to the aged, and parents are the pride of their children.*

7 *Arrogant lips are unsuited to a fool — how much worse lying lips to a ruler!*

8 *A bribe is a charm to the one who gives it; wherever he turns, he succeeds.*

9 *He who covers over an offense promotes love, but whoever repeats the matter separates close friends.*

10 *A rebuke impresses a man of discernment more than a hundred lashes a fool.*

11 *An evil man is bent only on rebellion; a merciless official will be sent against him.*

12 *Better to meet a bear robbed of her cubs than a fool in his folly.*

13 *If a man pays back evil for good, evil will never leave his house.*

14 *Starting a quarrel is like breaching a dam; so drop the matter before a dispute breaks out.*

15 *Acquitting the guilty and condemning the innocent — the* LORD *detests them both.*

16 *Of what use is money in the hand of a fool, since he has no desire to get wisdom?*

17 *A friend loves at all times, and a brother is born for adversity.*

18 *A man lacking in judgment strikes hands in pledge and puts up security for his neighbor.*

19 *He who loves a quarrel loves sin; he who builds a high gate invites destruction.*

PROVERBS 17

20 *A man of perverse heart does not prosper; he whose tongue is deceitful falls into trouble.*

21 *To have a fool for a son brings grief; there is no joy for the father of a fool.*

22 *A cheerful heart is good medicine, but a crushed spirit dries up the bones.*

23 *A wicked man accepts a bribe in secret to pervert the course of justice.*

24 *A discerning man keeps wisdom in view, but a fool's eyes wander to the ends of the earth.*

25 *A foolish son brings grief to his father and bitterness to the one who bore him.*

26 *It is not good to punish an innocent man, or to flog officials for their integrity.*

27 *A man of knowledge uses words with restraint, and a man of understanding is even-tempered.*

28 *Even a fool is thought wise if he keeps silent, and discerning if he holds his tongue.*

CHAPTER 17

SPECIAL FRIENDS

Proverbs 17:1-28

Key verse: "A friend loves at all times, and a brother is born for adversity."

— Proverbs 17:17

Several years ago, more than twenty now, I was passing through a difficult time in my life. Part of it was my fault, but at the time I couldn't see that. I simply felt betrayed, wounded by the church I had chosen to serve, rejected and misunderstood by my peers. It was a complicated situation, and there is nothing to be gained by delving into the painful details. Suffice it to say that were it not for some special friends I probably would not be in the ministry today.

For a number of months I lived in an ever-deepening depression. I covered it pretty well, but on the inside I felt as though I was dying. I loved God, but I didn't feel that I could trust Him. I loved the ministry, but there didn't seem to be any place for me. I guess I felt betrayed, yet at the same time I knew there was disobedience in my own heart. In desperation I turned to some special friends — Bob and Diana Arnold.

Thinking about them, I was almost overwhelmed. They were the first two converts of our ministry in Holly, Colorado. Many was the time Bob would call and say, "Diana has just baked a loaf of bread, and we've got a bottle of grape juice. Why don't you and Brenda come out and share Communion with us." Suddenly I wanted that, more than anything. I wanted that special relationship, with them, and with Jesus.

Bob and Diana, it turned out, were working on a farm in southwestern Kansas. After driving for most of the day and making a half a dozen phone calls, we finally located them. Though they hadn't heard from us in over two years, they were delighted when we showed up. It was as if we had never been apart.

On Saturday I bought a bottle of grape juice, and I asked Diana if she would bake some bread. After we got the kids to bed, we gathered around the scarred coffee table in their living room, just like old times, only now our roles were reversed. Many was the time I had cried and prayed with the two of them, now they wept and prayed with me.

I poured out my heart, I confessed everything — my hurt, my bitterness, even how close I had come to losing my faith. There were a lot of tears then, and a lot of love, and that farm house became a holy place, a sanctuary. We broke bread together, celebrated Holy Communion, and this broken man was made whole again.

The circumstances of my life didn't suddenly change. I still didn't have a place to preach, or a way of providing for my family, but those things seemed somehow inconsequential, especially in light of the holy thing which had just happened in my life. I was forgiven, I was among friends, I was back home at last, where I belonged. With God, my family and my friends I could face anything.

That is the heart of things, isn't it? — special friends! With them we can be content whatever the circumstances of our lives. In times of sorrow, they comfort us; in times of weakness, they strengthen us; and in times of success, they celebrate with us. It's true — "A friend loves at all times, and a brother is born for adversity."[1]

ACTION STEPS:

☐ Can you remember a time in your life when a special friend provided much needed support and encouragement? Take a few minutes now and write him a note, thanking him for his friendship and for his special support during that difficult time.

☐ Make a list of your special friends. Now pray for them one by one, being sensitive to any thoughts or impressions you may have while praying.

☐ If any special needs or concerns came to mind while you were praying, make a special effort to be a friend. Do what you can to help and encourage your friend in his hour of need.

THOUGHT FOR THE DAY:

"When I was in a foreign country once, I had to undergo an operation. The days immediately prior to it were extremely painful ones, and my mind and body were considerably worn by the ordeal. I felt terribly alone, entering a hospital in another land to be served by a physician who did not speak my language. On the morning of the day I was to enter the hospital, my wife attended church. She saw there a friend of ours who was a native of the country. 'Tell John,' he said to her, 'that I am holding him in my prayers.' I was standing at the bathroom sink when she told me, combing my hair. The impact of the words, in my nervous condition, was overpowering, and I burst into tears. I felt deliriously happy. To think he was praying for me. Somehow I was no longer alone. I was not far from home; this place was my home; any place would have been my home. I knew that then. I had seen to the heart of things."[2]

— John Killinger

PRAYER:

Lord, I started to pray, "Give me a friend like that." Instead I pray, "Make me a friend like that." In the name of Jesus I pray. Amen.

PROVERBS 18

1 *An unfriendly man pursues selfish ends; he defies all sound judgment.*

2 *A fool finds no pleasure in understanding but delights in airing his own opinions.*

3 *When wickedness comes, so does contempt, and with shame comes disgrace.*

4 *The words of a man's mouth are deep waters, but the fountain of wisdom is a bubbling brook.*

5 *It is not good to be partial to the wicked or to deprive the innocent of justice.*

6 *A fool's lips bring him strife, and his mouth invites a beating.*

7 *A fool's mouth is his undoing, and his lips are a snare to his soul.*

8 *The words of a gossip are like choice morsels; they go down to a man's inmost parts.*

9 *One who is slack in his work is brother to one who destroys.*

10 *The name of the* LORD *is a strong tower; the righteous run to it and are safe.*

11 *The wealth of the rich is their fortified city; they imagine it an unscalable wall.*

12 *Before his downfall a man's heart is proud, but humility comes before honor.*

13 *He who answers before listening — that is his folly and his shame.*

14 *A man's spirit sustains him in sickness, but a crushed spirit who can bear?*

15 *The heart of the discerning acquires knowledge; the ears of the wise seek it out.*

16 *A gift opens the way for the giver and ushers him into the presence of the great.*

17 *The first to present his case seems right, till another comes forward and questions him.*

18 *Casting the lot settles disputes and keeps strong opponents apart.*

19 *An offended brother is more unyielding than a fortified city, and disputes are like the barred gates of a citadel.*

20 *From the fruit of his mouth a man's stomach is filled; with the harvest from his lips he is satisfied.*

21 *The tongue has the power of life and death, and those who love it will eat its fruit.*

22 *He who finds a wife finds what is good and receives favor from the* LORD.

23 *A poor man pleads for mercy, but a rich man answers harshly.*

24 *A man of many companions may come to ruin, but there is a friend who sticks closer than a brother.*

CHAPTER 18

TRUST IN THE LORD

Proverbs 18:1-24

Key verse: "The name of the Lord is a strong tower; the righteous run to it and are safe."

— Proverbs 18:10

Nothing is more important than what a man believes about God. How he perceives Him will determine, to a significant degree, what he believes about himself and how he relates to others. It will also define his interpretation of life and the meaning of events. Never is his understanding of God more critical than in times of personal crisis. Consider, for example, the case of Judas Iscariot.

"When Judas, who had betrayed him, saw that Jesus was condemned, he was seized with remorse and returned the thirty silver coins to the chief priests and the elders. 'I have sinned,' he said, 'for I have betrayed innocent blood.'

"'What is that to us?' they replied. 'That's your responsibility.'

"So Judas threw the money into the temple and left. Then he went away and hanged himself."[1]

Judas clearly understood the magnitude of his sin, but he severely underestimated the grace of God. He could not live with the evil thing he had done, nor could he believe that God would forgive him. To his way of thinking, death was the only way out. It was both an escape and a desperate attempt to atone for his sin.

Judas's case is especially tragic because he had had the benefit of spending three years with Jesus. He had heard His teachings, witnessed His miracles and seen His redemptive love in action. How could he ever forget the woman caught in the very act of adultery or the words of Jesus when He said to her, "... ...neither do I condemn you...Go now and leave your life of sin'"?[2]

One can only conclude that the magnitude of Judas's treachery was such that his shameful guilt rendered these truths unreal. He remembered them, for who could ever forget, but to his way of thinking they had absolutely nothing to do with him. Tragically, he believed death at his own hand was somehow more merciful than the grace of God. What Judas believed about God determined his eternal fate in that critical hour.

David, on the other hand, never doubted the mercy of God, no matter how great his sin. Whatever his sin, whether it was adultery, or murder or prideful disobedience in numbering Israel's fighting men, David threw himself upon the mercy of God. Hear him as he cries to the Lord, "...'I have sinned greatly....I am in deep distress. Let us fall into the hands of the Lord, for his mercy is great....'"[3]

To David's way of thinking, God's grace was always greater than his sin. As a result, we remember him, not as an adulterer or a murderer, but as the sweet psalmist of Israel, a man after God's own heart and the earthly forefather of our Lord and Savior Jesus Christ.

The defining difference between David and Judas was their image of God. To David's way of thinking, "The Lord is a refuge for the oppressed, a stronghold in times of trouble."[4] He declared, "Those who know your name will trust in you, for you, Lord, have never forsaken those who seek you."[5]

To know God's name is not merely to know His title or what to call Him. A person's name, in the biblical sense, is the expression of his character, his nature. What David was saying then is that those of us who know God's character will put our trust in Him. Or as Solomon said, "The name of the Lord is a strong tower; the righteous run to it and are safe."[6]

ACTION STEPS:

☐ Copy Hebrews 11:11, Psalm 145:17, Deuteronomy 4:31, Exodus 34:6, Romans 4:21, Ephesians 3:20, Psalm 23:4, and Exodus 3:7,8 onto 3 X 5 cards and carry them with you in your pocket or briefcase.

☐ Make a point of reading through them two or three times a day for several days. Meditate on them until your heart and mind are saturated with their truth.

☐ Identify any situations in your life to which these Scriptures apply. What is God saying to you about these situations? Be specific.

THOUGHT FOR THE DAY:

"I know God is faithful so I trust Him.[7]
I know God is loving so I trust Him.[8]
I know God is merciful so I trust Him.[9]
I know God is compassionate so I trust Him.[10]
I know God is able so I trust Him.[11]
I know God is near so I trust Him.[12]
I know God is aware of my situation so I trust Him.[13]
I know God is involved in my situation so I trust Him."[14]
I know God is all powerful and trustworty so I trust Him.[15]

— A Private Journal

PRAYER:

Lord, You are my strength, my hope and my refuge, a very present help in time of trouble. I come boldly into Your presence, not because of who I am, but because of Who You are. I trust You with my life, with all that I am. In the name of Jesus I pray. Amen.

PROVERBS 19

1 *Better a poor man whose walk is blameless than a fool whose lips are perverse.*

2 *It is not good to have zeal without knowledge, nor to be hasty and miss the way.*

3 *A man's own folly ruins his life, yet his heart rages against the* LORD.

4 *Wealth brings many friends, but a poor man's friend deserts him.*

5 *A false witness will not go unpunished, and he who pours out lies will not go free.*

6 *Many curry favor with a ruler, and everyone is the friend of a man who gives gifts.*

7 *A poor man is shunned by all his relatives — how much more do his friends avoid him! Though he pursues them with pleading, they are nowhere to be found.*

8 *He who gets wisdom loves his own soul; he who cherishes understanding prospers.*

9 *A false witness will not go unpunished, and he who pours out lies will perish.*

10 *It is not fitting for a fool to live in luxury — how much worse for a slave to rule over princes!*

11 *A man's wisdom gives him patience; it is to his glory to overlook an offense.*

12 *A king's rage is like the roar of a lion, but his favor is like dew on the grass.*

13 *A foolish son is his father's ruin, and a quarrelsome wife is like a constant dripping.*

14 *Houses and wealth are inherited from parents, but a prudent wife is from the* LORD.

15 *Laziness brings on deep sleep, and the shiftless man goes hungry.*

16 *He who obeys instructions guards his life, but he who is contemptuous of his ways will die.*

17 *He who is kind to the poor lends to the* LORD, *and he will reward him for what he has done.*

18 *Discipline your son, for in that there is hope; do not be a willing party to his death.*

PROVERBS 19

19 *A hot-tempered man must pay the penalty; if you rescue him, you will have to do it again.*

20 *Listen to advice and accept instruction, and in the end you will be wise.*

21 *Many are the plans in a man's heart, but it is the* LORD's *purpose that prevails.*

22 *What a man desires is unfailing love; better to be poor than a liar.*

23 *The fear of the* LORD *leads to life: Then one rests content, untouched by trouble.*

24 *The sluggard buries his hand in the dish; he will not even bring it back to his mouth!*

25 *Flog a mocker, and the simple will learn prudence; rebuke a discerning man, and he will gain knowledge.*

26 *He who robs his father and drives out his mother is a son who brings shame and disgrace.*

27 *Stop listening to instruction, my son, and you will stray from the words of knowledge.*

28 *A corrupt witness mocks at justice, and the mouth of the wicked gulps down evil.*

29 *Penalties are prepared for mockers, and beatings for the backs of fools.*

CHAPTER 19

MISGUIDED ZEAL

Proverbs 19:1-29

Key verse: "It is not good to have zeal without knowledge, nor to be hasty and miss the way."
— Proverbs 19:2

Few things in life are more self-defeating than zeal without knowledge. It has claimed many a man, including presidents and kings, as well as military men of great renown. Numbered among its victims is Moses, the emancipator of Israel, and few have fallen so far as he.

Once a powerful prince in Pharaoh's palace, he becomes a fugitive tending sheep on the backside of the desert. Before his debacle he was a proud man, and why not? Among those who served in Pharaoh's courts none was as powerful as he, not in speech or in action.[1]

You wouldn't know it though, to look at him now. There's something almost apologetic about the way he carries himself, and when he speaks it is only with great difficulty.[2]

As you undoubtedly know, he is a Hebrew. Pharaoh's daughter adopted him and brought him to the palace after discovering him in a papyrus basket among some reeds along the bank of the Nile. His mother had hid him there rather than put him to death as Pharaoh's edict decreed. For a time it seemed as if he did everything he could to escape his Hebrew origins. He looked and dressed like an Egyptian prince, and he was educated in all the wisdom of the Egyptians. Everyone said that he was destined for a distinguished political career. Then something happened. No one seems to know exactly what, but he changed. He became sullen, withdrawn.

There were rumors that he was becoming obsessed with the Jewish problem, but I can't imagine that, not after he had worked so diligently to escape his past. Then when he was forty years old, he decided to visit his fellow Israelites. While at the work site, he saw one of them being mistreated by an Egyptian. In a fit of rage he attacked the Egyptian and killed him.

The next day Moses returned, only to discover two Hebrew slaves fighting. When he tried to intervene, the larger of the two men shoved him aside and said, "Who made you ruler and judge over us? Do you plan to kill me as you killed the Egyptian yesterday?"[3]

Moses tried to reason with him, tried to explain that God had placed him in a position of power so he could rescue his fellow Hebrews, but the man was not having any of it. By this time a crowd of slaves had gathered, so Moses appealed to them, but to no avail. They didn't trust him. As far as they were concerned, he was a traitor to his own people.

Once Moses made his intentions known, his days were numbered. Pharaoh had ears everywhere, and it was only a matter of time until he learned of Moses' clandestine meeting with the Hebrew slaves. As you might expect, he immediately issued orders to have Moses arrested and put to death. Luckily, someone warned Moses, and he escaped with his life. He fled to Midian where he married the daughter of a priest and became a shepherd tending her father's sheep.

The thing that broke Moses' heart, or so I am told, was not Pharaoh's attempt to take his life, but the rejection he suffered at the hands of his own people. In retrospect he was probably being naive, but he was absolutely convinced that it was his destiny to free the Hebrew slaves. So sure was he that the God of his fathers, the God of Abraham, Isaac, and Jacob, had called him to set them free that he was willing to risk everything. When they refused to follow him, he lost his faith, not only in God, but in himself as well. From that moment forward he was a broken man.

What can we learn from all of this? First: Planning must precede action. Apparently Moses was so anxious to be about the Lord's business that he acted without a prepared plan. This is a common mistake among those who have zeal without knowledge. Having little patience for planning, and absolutely no time or interest in dealing with details, they rush ahead without considering the consequences. They are men of action, or perhaps I should say reaction, and they simply assume that everyone else shares their vision and accepts their leadership — which is seldom the case. The resulting disaster often leaves them broken and embittered. As the wise man said, "A man's own folly ruins his life, yet his heart rages against the Lord."[4]

The second thing we learn is that sincerity is not enough, nor is zeal or even good intentions. Moses had all of these, and he still failed. Only God knows how much damage has been done by immature and overanxious believers, not only to the cause of Christ but to themselves as well. The secret of success in God's service is God's work in God's way in God's time!

And finally — the greatest lesson of all — there is no failure that God cannot redeem! Moses got a second chance, and this time he succeeded. He challenged Egypt's military might and won; he confronted Pharaoh and negotiated the release of two million slaves, and then led them to freedom. Subsequently, he gave them a system of government, a theocracy. He organized their religion, designed and built their place of worship and defined their God for them. For forty years, he was their spiritual father, their priest, their prophet, their general and their prime minister. In addition, he penned the first five books of the Bible, including the Ten Commandments which, to this day, are the foundation for moral order in our society.

If you've failed, don't despair, not even if you've made a real mess of your life. "...God's gifts and his call are irrevocable."[5] That is to say, there is nothing you can do, no willful disobedience, no foolish mistake, that will cause God to revoke His call on your life. "For though a righteous man falls seven times, he rises again...."[6]

ACTION STEPS:

☐ Examine the way you make decisions. Do you think things through or do you allow your unbridled enthusiasm to distort your judgment?

Do you discuss your plans with your wife or anyone else who might be involved, or do you simply present them your decision?

☐ If you have recently made a bad decision, examine the whole process to see what you can learn from it. Where did you go wrong? What will you do different next time?

☐ If you have recently made a wise decision, examine the whole process to see what you can learn from it. What did you do right? What principles will you use the next time you have an important decision to make?

THOUGHT FOR THE DAY:

"Press on: Nothing in the world can take the place of persistence. Talent will not; nothing is more common than unsuccessful individuals with talent. Genius will not; unrewarded genius is almost a proverb. Education will not; the world is full of educated derelicts. Persistence and determination alone are omnipotent."[7]

— Ray Kroc

PRAYER:

Lord, I am so thankful that You used imperfect men to accomplish Your purposes. Without their failures, their successes would intimidate me. Their humanness, their mistakes, give me hope. If You could use men like them, then maybe You can use a man like me too. Use me for Your purposes, O Lord, I pray. In Jesus' name. Amen.

PROVERBS 20

1 *Wine is a mocker and beer a brawler; whoever is led astray by them is not wise.*

2 *A king's wrath is like the roar of a lion; he who angers him forfeits his life.*

3 *It is to a man's honor to avoid strife, but every fool is quick to quarrel.*

4 *A sluggard does not plow in season; so at harvest time he looks but finds nothing.*

5 *The purposes of a man's heart are deep waters, but a man of understanding draws them out.*

6 *Many a man claims to have unfailing love, but a faithful man who can find?*

7 *The righteous man leads a blameless life; blessed are his children after him.*

8 *When a king sits on his throne to judge, he winnows out all evil with his eyes.*

9 *Who can say, "I have kept my heart pure; I am clean and without sin"?*

10 *Differing weights and differing measures — the LORD detests them both.*

11 *Even a child is known by his actions, by whether his conduct is pure and right.*

12 *Ears that hear and eyes that see — the LORD has made them both.*

13 *Do not love sleep or you will grow poor; stay awake and you will have food to spare.*

14 *"It's no good, it's no good!" says the buyer; then off he goes and boasts about his purchase.*

15 *Gold there is, and rubies in abundance, but lips that speak knowledge are a rare jewel.*

16 *Take the garment of one who puts up security for a stranger; hold it in pledge if he does it for a wayward woman.*

17 *Food gained by fraud tastes sweet to a man, but he ends up with a mouth full of gravel.*

18 *Make plans by seeking advice; if you wage war, obtain guidance.*

19 *A gossip betrays a confidence; so avoid a man who talks too much.*
20 *If a man curses his father or mother, his lamp will be snuffed out in pitch darkness.*
21 *An inheritance quickly gained at the beginning will not be blessed at the end.*
22 *Do not say, "I'll pay you back for this wrong!" Wait for the* LORD, *and he will deliver you.*
23 *The* LORD *detests differing weights, and dishonest scales do not please him.*
24 *A man's steps are directed by the* LORD. *How then can anyone understand his own way?*
25 *It is a trap for a man to dedicate something rashly and only later to consider his vows.*
26 *A wise king winnows out the wicked; he drives the threshing wheel over them.*
27 *The lamp of the* LORD *searches the spirit of a man; it searches out his inmost being.*
28 *Love and faithfulness keep a king safe; through love his throne is made secure.*
29 *The glory of young men is their strength, gray hair the splendor of the old.*
30 *Blows and wounds cleanse away evil, and beatings purge the inmost being.*

CHAPTER 20

FRIENDS

Proverbs 20:1-30

Key verse: "A gossip betrays a confidence; so avoid a man who talks too much."

— Proverbs 20:19

Every man needs a friend, someone in whom he can confide. There is simply no way to overstate the tremendous need he has to be really listened to, to be taken seriously, to be understood. Without that kind of relationship, he will never experience his full potential as a human being and a man of God.

According to Dr. Paul Tournier, the eminent Swiss psychiatrist and Christian thinker, "No one can develop freely in this world and find a full life without feeling understood by at least one person. Misunderstood, he loses his self-confidence, he loses his faith in life or even in God."[1]

Yet, few men have the kind of friendships in which they can let down their guard and truly be themselves. The reasons are both cultural and experiential.

"According to Elliot Engel of North Carolina State, the male twosome is designed more for combat than comfort. Men are expected to compete, whether the setting is the tennis court or the law court."[2] Joel Block, a Long Island psychologist, concurs. He says that the growing-up message programmed into men is, "Show any weakness, and we'll clobber you with it."[3]

Those who manage to overcome these cultural hang-ups and build a friendship based on mutual trust, transparency and vulnerability experience personal wholeness and a depth of self-knowledge uncommon among men. Yet, such a relationship is not without its risks. Not infrequently the man who enters into such a friendship finds his trust betrayed. He tells his friend of the difficulties he is experiencing with his supervisor, only to discover that his friend uses that information for his own advancement. Or he confides that he is having trouble with sex in his marriage, and his friend "jokingly" replies, "Well, perhaps I ought to come over and help you out."

Such betrayal only reinforces his cultural training, and after one or two such experiences most men learn to keep their own counsel. Well it has been said that women start out as strangers and end up as sisters, while men start as strangers and end as swordsmen.

Is there a solution, an answer, a way for us men to build deep and meaningful friendships without risking it all? Yes, but only if we will accept the counsel of Scripture. The wise man instructs us to choose our friends carefully. He writes, "A gossip betrays a confidence; so avoid a man who talks too much."[4]

Never trust a man who tells you another man's secret. If he betrays that man's confidence, he is likely to betray yours as well. Such a man reveals the things told to him in confidence as a way of proving his importance. The deepest issues of another person's life become the currency he uses to advance himself. Beware of such a friend.

The Bible says, "The purposes of a man's heart are deep waters, but a man of understanding draws them out."[5] In other words, a man's motives are not always as pure as they first appear. A wise man withholds judgment until he has had opportunity to make sure that his potential friend's actions match his words.

The real key to building a true friendship is caution — not suspicion, but caution. Give your new friend a small piece of your heart. If he treats it with respect and understanding, or better yet, if he reciprocates, then share a little more of yourself. In this way, you can build a genuine friendship without risking your whole heart at once. As Solomon observed, "A righteous man is cautious in friendship...."[6]

ACTION STEPS:

*Consider this: If you were to discover that your wife was having an affair or your teenage son was doing drugs, who could you talk to?

Who could you call in that terrible moment and share your deepest hurt?

*If you cannot think of anyone other than your pastor and/or some other professional, then you probably do not have the kind of friendships you need in order to become all that God has called you to be. Examine your life to see if you can determine why you lack that kind of in-depth relationship. Be specific.

*Make a list of the changes you are willing to make to develop the kind of friendships we've been talking about. Be specific.

THOUGHT FOR THE DAY:

"...no one comes to know himself through introspection, or in the solitude of his personal diary. Rather, it is in dialogue, in his meeting with other persons. It is only by expressing his conviction to others that he becomes really conscious of them. He who would see himself clearly must open up to a confidant freely chosen and worthy of such trust."[7]

— Dr. Paul Tournier

PRAYER:

Lord, I am a blessed man. You have given me some very special friends. In my darkest hour they have been my strength and my support. They have stood with me, believed in me when I could no longer believe in myself. Without them, I don't think I could have made it. Now I ask You to make me a friend like that to someone who needs the strength of friendship in the midnight hour of his life. In Jesus' name I pray. Amen.

PROVERBS 21

1 *The king's heart is in the hand of the* LORD*; he directs it like a watercourse wherever he pleases.*

2 *All a man's ways seem right to him, but the* LORD *weighs the heart.*

3 *To do what is right and just is more acceptable to the* LORD *than sacrifice.*

4 *Haughty eyes and a proud heart, the lamp of the wicked, are sin!*

5 *The plans of the diligent lead to profit as surely as haste leads to poverty.*

6 *A fortune made by a lying tongue is a fleeting vapor and a deadly snare.*

7 *The violence of the wicked will drag them away, for they refuse to do what is right.*

8 *The way of the guilty is devious, but the conduct of the innocent is upright.*

9 *Better to live on a corner of the roof than share a house with a quarrelsome wife.*

10 *The wicked man craves evil; his neighbor gets no mercy from him.*

11 *When a mocker is punished, the simple gain wisdom; when a wise man is instructed, he gets knowledge.*

12 *The Righteous One takes note of the house of the wicked and brings the wicked to ruin.*

13 *If a man shuts his ears to the cry of the poor, he too will cry out and not be answered.*

14 *A gift given in secret soothes anger, and a bribe concealed in the cloak pacifies great wrath.*

15 *When justice is done, it brings joy to the righteous but terror to evildoers.*

16 *A man who strays from the path of understanding comes to rest in the company of the dead.*

17 *He who loves pleasure will become poor; whoever loves wine and oil will never be rich.*

18 *The wicked become a ransom for the righteous, and the unfaithful for the upright.*

PROVERBS 21

19 *Better to live in a desert than with a quarrelsome and ill-tempered wife.*

20 *In the house of the wise are stores of choice food and oil, but a foolish man devours all he has.*

21 *He who pursues righteousness and love finds life, prosperity and honor.*

22 *A wise man attacks the city of the mighty and pulls down the stronghold in which they trust.*

23 *He who guards his mouth and his tongue keeps himself from calamity.*

24 *The proud and arrogant man — "Mocker" is his name; he behaves with overweening pride.*

25 *The sluggard's craving will be the death of him, because his hands refuse to work.*

26 *All day long he craves for more, but the righteous give without sparing.*

27 *The sacrifice of the wicked is detestable — how much more so when brought with evil intent!*

28 *A false witness will perish, and whoever listens to him will be destroyed forever.*

29 *A wicked man puts up a bold front, but an upright man gives thought to his ways.*

30 *There is no wisdom, no insight, no plan that can succeed against the* LORD.

31 *The horse is made ready for the day of battle, but victory rests with the* LORD.

CHAPTER 21

AN UPRIGHT MAN

Proverbs 21:1-31

Key verse: "A wicked man puts up a bold front, but an upright man gives thought to his ways."

— Proverbs 21:29

The man of the world is concerned about appearances — wearing the right clothes, driving the right kind of car, knowing the right people, even working for the right company. He wants to be politically correct in everything he does. To him, image is "the name of the game," and he is constantly testing the wind to make sure he is in step with the "in" crowd. As far as he's concerned, first impressions are everything.

The spiritual man — what Proverbs calls the "upright man" — is concerned with integrity. He recognizes the value of first impressions, but he is more concerned about the long haul. For him, the important question is, do I wear well? Congruity is important too. What he appears to be and what he truly is must be one and the same. To his way of thinking, substance is more important than show.

When I think of an upright man, my mind immediately turns to my Uncle Ernie. He was not a great man as the world counts greatness. He was never the pastor of a large church, he never wrote a book, nor did he ever make a name for himself. He was, however, a special man, a throwback to an earlier age when the measure of a man was determined by the quality of his character rather than the power of his personality. In truth, he was one of those men who "wore well" — that is, the longer you knew him, the more you appreciated him.

If you don't look beneath the surface, Uncle Ernie's life appears rather insignificant, but on a deeper level it has eternal value. Only God knows how many men and women received Jesus Christ as their Savior as a result of his witness, and who can measure the value of a single soul? A number of young men got their start in the ministry with his help, including me. He was a special friend and my first spiritual mentor.

When I was just a boy preacher of sixteen, I telephoned him to ask if I could preach a revival meeting in his church. Only now, these many years later, do I realize how presumptuous that was. Nonetheless, he opened his pulpit to me.

Before the first service he offered to critique my sermons. Of course, I agreed, not because I felt a need for his expertise, but simply because I knew of no way to tell him that it wouldn't be necessary without appearing immodest.

My first sermon was more legalism than Gospel, but what I lacked in theology I more than made up for with feverish enthusiasm. With a zeal that now seems frightening, I preached about the Great White Throne Judgment. In truth, I dangled those poor saints over hell on a rotting stick. When I had finally finished, I was quite pleased with myself.

Uncle Ernie didn't seem eager to critique my sermon, and who could blame him? I mean, how do you tell your sixteen-year-old nephew that he is one of the finest preachers you have ever heard without exposing him to the deadliest of all ministerial temptations — pride? Imagine my chagrin when we finally entered his study, late the next day, and he preceded to dismantle my sermonic masterpiece with surgical skill.

When he had finally finished, I was absolutely devastated. Although it was one of the most painful experiences of my life, I can truthfully say that it was also one of the most helpful. The foundations for all that I am today, as a preacher and as a minister, were laid that afternoon. Needless to say, I will be forever grateful that Uncle Ernie cared enough to risk offending me in order to get me started right.

Today Uncle Ernie has gone to be with the Lord, but even in death his ministry lives on. He had a profound influence on my brother Don and his decision to become a missionary. Another nephew, Orville Stewart, is a pastor, and Uncle Ernie's ministry lives on in his work also. Of course, anything I do, and whatever influence I have, is his as well. To this day he remains my model for ministry — an upright man — a man of integrity.

ACTION STEPS:

☐ Consider this: When you think of an upright man, who do you think of? What characteristics do you most admire in his life?

☐ In prayer, examine your own life. Is it built on show or substance? If people really knew you the way you know yourself, would they still respect and admire you? Why?

☐ Confess any areas of inconsistency to God and ask Him to help you become a man of integrity. Share your confession with a trusted friend and invite him to hold you accountable.

THOUGHT FOR THE DAY:

"The measure of a man's real character is what he would do, if he knew he would never be found out."[1]

— Macaulay

PRAYER:

Lord, I want to be an upright man, a man of integrity. I often fall short of this high ideal, but I refuse to give up. With Your help I will be a godly man, not only in appearance, but in heart and mind as well. In the name of Jesus I pray. Amen.

PROVERBS 22

1 *A good name is more desirable than great riches; to be esteemed is better than silver or gold.*

2 *Rich and poor have this in common: The* LORD *is the Maker of them all.*

3 *A prudent man sees danger and takes refuge, but the simple keep going and suffer for it.*

4 *Humility and the fear of the* LORD *bring wealth and honor and life.*

5 *In the paths of the wicked lie thorns and snares, but he who guards his soul stays far from them.*

6 *Train a child in the way he should go, and when he is old he will not turn from it.*

7 *The rich rule over the poor, and the borrower is servant to the lender.*

8 *He who sows wickedness reaps trouble, and the rod of his fury will be destroyed.*

9 *A generous man will himself be blessed, for he shares his food with the poor.*

10 *Drive out the mocker, and out goes strife; quarrels and insults are ended.*

11 *He who loves a pure heart and whose speech is gracious will have the king for his friend.*

12 *The eyes of the* LORD *keep watch over knowledge, but he frustrates the words of the unfaithful.*

13 *The sluggard says, "There is a lion outside!" or, "I will be murdered in the streets!"*

14 *The mouth of an adulteress is a deep pit; he who is under the* LORD*'s wrath will fall into it.*

15 *Folly is bound up in the heart of a child, but the rod of discipline will drive it far from him.*

16 *He who oppresses the poor to increase his wealth and he who gives gifts to the rich—both come to poverty.*

17 *Pay attention and listen to the sayings of the wise; apply your heart to what I teach,*

18 *for it is pleasing when you keep them in your heart and have all of them ready on your lips.*

19 *So that your trust may be in the* LORD, *I teach you today, even you.*

20 *Have I not written thirty sayings for you, sayings of counsel and knowledge,*

21 *teaching you true and reliable words, so that you can give sound answers to him who sent you?*

22 *Do not exploit the poor because they are poor and do not crush the needy in court,*

23 *for the* LORD *will take up their case and will plunder those who plunder them.*

24 *Do not make friends with a hot-tempered man, do not associate with one easily angered,*

25 *or you may learn his ways and get yourself ensnared.*

26 *Do not be a man who strikes hands in pledge or puts up security for debts;*

27 *if you lack the means to pay, your very bed will be snatched from under you.*

28 *Do not move an ancient boundary stone set up by your forefathers.*

29 *Do you see a man skilled in his work? He will serve before kings; he will not serve before obscure men.*

CHAPTER 22

THE STEPS OF A RIGHTEOUS MAN

Proverbs 22:1-29

Key verse: "Do you see a man skilled in his work? He will serve before kings; he will not serve before obscure men."

— Proverbs 22:29

In the competitive world of business where it is every man for himself, where only the most ruthless succeed, it is a great comfort to know that God has a plan for our lives. While other men claw and scratch their way to the top, the believer simply rests in the knowledge that "The Lord will fulfill his purpose for me...."[1] That is not to say that he is complacent or lackadaisical, for he is not. His work ethic comes from the Scriptures: "Whatever you do, work at it with all your heart, as working for the Lord, not for men."[2]

The difference between the work habits of the unbeliever and those of the believer is not so much one of energy or effort, but of motive. The unbeliever works to get ahead, to advance his career. The believer works to please the Lord. The unbeliever depends on his own ingenuity to advance his career. The believer trusts the faithfulness of God. He knows that if he is faithful over a few things, he will be made ruler over many things.[3] As the wise man said, "Do you see a man skilled in his work? He will serve before kings; he will not serve before obscure men."[4]

More than anyone I know, Clifton Taulbert epitomizes this truth. As a black boy growing up in the Mississippi Delta in the 1950s, he knew the harsh reality of racism, but he refused to allow it to make him bitter. After graduating from high school, he boarded the train heading north. Armed with his faith in God and the love of his family, he set out to fulfill his destiny. Little did he know the plans God had for his life.

Following four years in the Air Force, the last two of which were spent serving in the prestigious 89th Presidential Wing, he enrolled at Oral

Roberts University where he completed his undergraduate studies in business. When the Bank of Oklahoma hired him, he became the first black bank officer in the history of Tulsa. While at BOK he completed work on his master's degree from Southwest Graduate School of Banking at Southern Methodist University.

After leaving the Bank of Oklahoma, he founded Freemont Corporation, a diversified marketing and consulting company. Once again the favor of God blessed his efforts, and he experienced a number of significant successes. Among the most notable was the establishment of a worldwide government market for the Stair Master exercise equipment. Also during this time, he became president of Spike Sports Drink, the first Afro-American-owned sports drink company.

During these years Cliff was a part of Christian Chapel, the congregation I served as senior pastor. Although he was obviously a gifted leader, he had a true servant's heart. For a number of years he served as the head usher at Christian Chapel, a job at which he excelled. He constantly reached out to young men and poured his life into them. Although we shared lunch from time to time, he seldom talked about his business or his dreams. Instead, we talked about the things of the Lord.

For all his success, Cliff never forgot his roots, nor the extended family that gave him his identity. He only regretted that his own children would never know the rich heritage that had been his. These voices from the past seemed too significant to simply let pass away, so he began writing a book. *Once Upon A Time When We Were Colored* (Council Oak) was originally intended simply to acquaint his children with their family history, but soon its heartwarming appeal made it an international bestseller.

It was one of the first foreign books openly provided to Nelson Mandela by the U.S. State Department following his release from prison. It became an interdisciplinary text for high schools across the country and was read in its entirety on National Public Radio.

Universities recognized it as a first-person resource for doctoral theses on Southern culture. Invitations for public appearances and speaking engagements poured in. Soon Cliff was traveling and lecturing internationally. For all his success, he remained the same Cliff, and most of us at Christian Chapel only heard rumors of the many awards which came his way.

In 1992 he published a sequel titled *The Last Train North* (Council Oak). It too had the same heartwarming appeal that had made *Once Upon A Time When We Were Colored* so successful. *The Last Train North* won Cliff a Pulitzer Prize nomination, as well as a host of other awards. He became the first Afro-American to win the Mississippi Institute of Arts and Letters Award for nonfiction as the 1993 nonfiction co-winner. He was named 1992 Double Day (First Light) Author and was awarded the 1993 Mississippi Library Association Award.

Cliff's achievements would be significant for any man, but for a black boy born to a gambling man and a high school girl, and who was reared in the Mississippi Delta where racism was a religion, they are nothing short of unbelievable. To Cliff's way of thinking, his success is truly God's doing and, as such, it should be an inspiration to all of us who are trusting God to fulfill His purposes in our lives.

ACTION STEPS:

☐ Memorize Proverbs 22:29 and Psalm 138:7,8. Meditate on these verses until they become core convictions in your life.

☐ Deliberately surrender your life unconditionally to the Lord. Ask Him to fulfill His purposes in your life. Make this a daily prayer.

THOUGHT FOR THE DAY:

"God has a history of using the insignificant to accomplish the impossible."[5]

— Richard Exley

PRAYER:

Lord, sometimes it is hard to trust You with my life and my career. I am afraid that Your plans for me are not big enough. Forgive me, Lord, for thinking that I know better than You what is best for me. Now I pray, "Not my will, but Your will be done." In Jesus' name. Amen.

PROVERBS 23

1 *When you sit to dine with a ruler, note well what is before you,*
2 *and put a knife to your throat if you are given to gluttony.*
3 *Do not crave his delicacies, for that food is deceptive.*
4 *Do not wear yourself out to get rich; have the wisdom to show restraint.*
5 *Cast but a glance at riches, and they are gone, for they will surely sprout wings and fly off to the sky like an eagle.*
6 *Do not eat the food of a stingy man, do not crave his delicacies;*
7 *for he is the kind of man who is always thinking about the cost. "Eat and drink," he says to you, but his heart is not with you.*
8 *You will vomit up the little you have eaten and will have wasted your compliments.*
9 *Do not speak to a fool, for he will scorn the wisdom of your words.*
10 *Do not move an ancient boundary stone or encroach on the fields of the fatherless,*
11 *for their Defender is strong; he will take up their case against you.*
12 *Apply your heart to instruction and your ears to words of knowledge.*
13 *Do not withhold discipline from a child; if you punish him with the rod, he will not die.*
14 *Punish him with the rod and save his soul from death.*
15 *My son, if your heart is wise, then my heart will be glad;*
16 *my inmost being will rejoice when your lips speak what is right.*
17 *Do not let your heart envy sinners, but always be zealous for the fear of the* LORD.
18 *There is surely a future hope for you, and your hope will not be cut off.*
19 *Listen, my son, and be wise, and keep your heart on the right path.*
20 *Do not join those who drink too much wine or gorge themselves on meat,*
21 *for drunkards and gluttons become poor, and drowsiness clothes them in rags.*
22 *Listen to your father, who gave you life, and do not despise your mother when she is old.*

PROVERBS 23

23 *Buy the truth and do not sell it; get wisdom, discipline and understanding.*

24 *The father of a righteous man has great joy; he who has a wise son delights in him.*

25 *May your father and mother be glad; may she who gave you birth rejoice!*

26 *My son, give me your heart and let your eyes keep to my ways,*

27 *for a prostitute is a deep pit and a wayward wife is a narrow well.*

28 *Like a bandit she lies in wait, and multiplies the unfaithful among men.*

29 *Who has woe? Who has sorrow? Who has strife? Who has complaints? Who has needless bruises? Who has bloodshot eyes?*

30 *Those who linger over wine, who go to sample bowls of mixed wine.*

31 *Do not gaze at wine when it is red, when it sparkles in the cup, when it goes down smoothly!*

32 *In the end it bites like a snake and poisons like a viper.*

33 *Your eyes will see strange sights and your mind imagine confusing things.*

34 *You will be like one sleeping on the high seas, lying on top of the rigging.*

35 *"They hit me," you will say, "but I'm not hurt! They beat me, but I don't feel it! When will I wake up so I can find another drink?"*

CHAPTER 23

LOVE AND DISCIPLINE

Proverbs 23:1-35

Key verses: "Do not withhold discipline from a child; if you punish him with the rod, he will not die. Punish him with the rod and save his soul from death."

— Proverbs 23:13,14

As men and fathers, one of our primary responsibilities is the nurture and discipline of our children. Failing here, we face the most painful consequences. Of all our shortcomings, none is more potentially devastating. Even now America is reaping the firstfruits of this bitter harvest. Juvenile violence is increasing at an alarming rate. According to a recent study, one in every five twelfth-graders was injured as a result of violence in school during the past year.[1]

As Chuck Colson points out, "It wasn't so long ago that the weapons of choice among students were rubber bands and spitballs. Today if you check their bags, you're likely to find everything from handguns to knives, razor blades, brass knuckles, and broken beer bottles."[2] No wonder many junior and senior high schools now utilize metal detectors and security guards in an attempt to keep their halls safe.

With our penchant for affixing blame rather than correcting problems, we rush around demanding to know who fouled up. In truth, there is enough blame to go around. The educational system must shoulder its share of the blame for failing in its responsibility to include character education in its curriculum. The Supreme Court bears no little responsibility for issuing a series of decisions that severely undermine school discipline. But no one bears more responsibility than parents. Because we have refused to discipline our children at home, we have made it almost impossible for anyone else to discipline them.

Let me share an incident which is a case in point. My father and I are enjoying the last of our ice cream when a young mother and her two children take the table next to us. They are an attractive family — she in a glistening white jogging suit and running shoes, the kids in designer jeans and fashionably sloppy pullovers. From all appearances they are a typical yuppie family — young, professional and politically correct.

As soon as they are seated, the little guy, who looks to be six or seven years old, thrusts his straw deep into his chocolate shake and sucks hard. With a malevolent gleam in his eye, he withdraws the straw, turns toward his mother and blows. In an instant the front of her white jogging suit is covered with a chocolate mess. I can't bear to watch so I turn my head and wait for the explosion. Imagine my chagrin when I hear her say, "Don't do that, honey."

Don't do that, honey?

What kind of response is that to the willful destructiveness her son has just wrought? I risk a glance toward their table only to discover that she is calmly dabbing at the chocolate mess now running down the front of her jacket. Of course, her stern reprimand has properly terrified her mischievous son. Meekly he returns the straw to his shake. Meekly he reloads, and meekly he deposits a second load full in his sister's face.

I watch in amazement as his mother calmly leans across the table and begins to wipe chocolate off of her daughter's face. Once more she says, with pseudo sweetness, "Honey, I told you not to do that. Now just look what you've done to Sissy." The kid surveys the damage, gives his mother a satisfied smirk, then turns his attention once more to his shake.

At this point Dad and I make our exit. Once in the car we stare at one another dumbly. Finally, I ask, "Did you see what I just saw?" Nodding his head, Dad replies, "If you're talking about that six-year-old terrorizing his mother and sister, I saw it. What that kid needs is a good spanking!"

Apparently that boy's mother is into the philosophy of permissive parenting. Corporal punishment is out, and allowing the child to fully vent his feelings is in — we don't want to thwart his creativity, do we?

That may sound good on paper, but real life is an altogether different matter. Already this mother is reaping the consequences of her misguided decisions, and it is only a matter of time until her son graduates to more serious weapons. In truth, her troubles are just starting. Her dilemma should come as no surprise to those of us familiar with the Scriptures. Proverbs declares, "The rod of correction imparts wisdom, but a child left to himself disgraces his mother."[3]

Contrary to what the psychological gurus say, corporal punishment is not an act of violence, but of discipline. Administered consistently, and balanced with unconditional love, it teaches children respect for God's authority and for the authority of those He has placed over them. When parents refuse to discipline their children for disrespectful and destructive behavior, they teach them to disregard authority and the rights of others.

If you would fulfill your responsibilities as a father, you must commit to the biblical principles of child rearing, including discipline. Biblical discipline is consistent, the rules are clearly defined and the punishment is appropriate. Discipline must be administered according to the child's behavior, not according to the parent's mood or some other personal whim. Children need to know that every time they are disobedient, they will be punished. This is not cruelty but love, tough love. True biblical discipline is always an expression of love, not anger, and has the child's best interest at heart.

"Discipline without love is tyrannical and produces children who will grow up to be both hostile and afraid. Love without discipline is permissive and trains children to be selfish and obnoxious. But when unconditional love and consistent discipline are combined, they produce children who are emotionally healthy and well adjusted."[4]

ACTION STEPS:

☐ Examine your philosophy of discipline. Is it based on Scripture, or on the current psychological model? Please explain.

☐ Rate yourself as a disciplinarian using a scale of one to ten with ten being excellent. Consider such factors as consistency, fairness, appropriateness and love. Ask your wife to rate you as well and then together discuss your answers.

☐ Ask yourself what areas, if any, you need to improve in. Be specific.

THOUGHT FOR THE DAY:

"The Bible offers a consistent foundation on which to build an effective philosophy of parent-child relationships. It is my belief that we have departed from the standard which was clearly outlined in both the Old and New Testaments, and that deviation is costing us a heavy toll in the form of social turmoil. Self-control, human kindness, respect, and peacefulness can again be manifest in America if we will return to this ultimate resource in our homes and schools."[5]

— Dr. James Dobson

PRAYER:

Lord, being a parent isn't easy. I constantly find myself reacting instead of responding. I'm too busy, too tired, too preoccupied, too something.... Forgive me, Lord. My children deserve better, they need more. Help me to become the father they need, the one You have called me to be. In the name of Jesus I pray. Amen.

PROVERBS 24

1 *Do not envy wicked men, do not desire their company;*

2 *for their hearts plot violence, and their lips talk about making trouble.*

3 *By wisdom a house is built, and through understanding it is established;*

4 *through knowledge its rooms are filled with rare and beautiful treasures.*

5 *A wise man has great power, and a man of knowledge increases strength;*

6 *for waging war you need guidance, and for victory many advisers.*

7 *Wisdom is too high for a fool; in the assembly at the gate he has nothing to say.*

8 *He who plots evil will be known as a schemer.*

9 *The schemes of folly are sin, and men detest a mocker.*

10 *If you falter in times of trouble, how small is your strength!*

11 *Rescue those being led away to death; hold back those staggering toward slaughter.*

12 *If you say, "But we knew nothing about this," does not he who weighs the heart perceive it? Does not he who guards your life know it? Will he not repay each person according to what he has done?*

13 *Eat honey, my son, for it is good; honey from the comb is sweet to your taste.*

14 *Know also that wisdom is sweet to your soul; if you find it, there is a future hope for you, and your hope will not be cut off.*

15 *Do not lie in wait like an outlaw against a righteous man's house, do not raid his dwelling place;*

16 *for though a righteous man falls seven times, he rises again, but the wicked are brought down by calamity.*

17 *Do not gloat when your enemy falls; when he stumbles, do not let your heart rejoice,*

18 *or the* LORD *will see and disapprove and turn his wrath away from him.*

19 *Do not fret because of evil men or be envious of the wicked,*

20 *for the evil man has no future hope, and the lamp of the wicked will be snuffed out.*

21 *Fear the* LORD *and the king, my son, and do not join with the rebellious,*

22 *for those two will send sudden destruction upon them, and who knows what calamities they can bring?*

23 *These also are sayings of the wise: To show partiality in judging is not good:*

24 *Whoever says to the guilty, "You are innocent"— peoples will curse him and nations denounce him.*

25 *But it will go well with those who convict the guilty, and rich blessing will come upon them.*

26 *An honest answer is like a kiss on the lips.*

27 *Finish your outdoor work and get your fields ready; after that, build your house.*

28 *Do not testify against your neighbor without cause, or use your lips to deceive.*

29 *Do not say, "I'll do to him as he has done to me; I'll pay that man back for what he did."*

30 *I went past the field of the sluggard, past the vineyard of the man who lacks judgment;*

31 *thorns had come up everywhere, the ground was covered with weeds, and the stone wall was in ruins.*

32 *I applied my heart to what I observed and learned a lesson from what I saw:*

33 *A little sleep, a little slumber, a little folding of the hands to rest —*

34 *and poverty will come on you like a bandit and scarcity like an armed man.*

CHAPTER 24

THE POWER OF PERSEVERANCE

Proverbs 24:1-34

Key verse: "For though a righteous man falls seven times, he rises again, but the wicked are brought down by calamity."

— Proverbs 24:16

Failure hurts! It's disappointing, embarrassing, humiliating. Say what you will about its benefits, say it builds character, say it teaches compassion, the fact is that it still hurts. And if you are like most people, when you fail, you are inundated with doubts about your intelligence, your abilities and your worth. You are embarrassed and tempted to give up. Don't! At least not until you've considered God's record for transforming failures, for turning life's misfits and rejects into dynamic men and women of worth!

"When Nathaniel Hawthorne lost his position in the Custom House at Salem, Massachusetts, he came home utterly defeated to tell his wife that he was a complete failure. To his amazement she greeted his dismal news with delight, saying, 'Now you can write your book.' So he sat down and wrote *The Scarlet Letter*, still considered by many critics as the greatest novel ever written in our country."[1]

"Philip Brooks, the noted Episcopal minister who died in the 1890s, had planned to be a teacher and had prepared himself for the profession of teaching. But he failed so ingloriously that he became despondent. Then he prepared himself for the ministry. In this calling he made a huge success."[2]

What am I trying to say? Just this: failure isn't final. The list of men in the Bible who failed and yet went on to greatness is long and impressive. Joseph was a slave and a prisoner before ascending to power in Egypt. Moses was a murderer and a fugitive before he became the emancipator of the Israelites. David committed adultery, yet we remember him as a man after God's own heart. Peter denied Jesus, yet he became a noted apostle and ultimately died a martyr rather than renounce his Lord. Saul of Tarsus was a zealous persecutor of the Church, yet after his conversion he became the foremost missionary in the early Church and the most prolific writer of the New Testament.

Secular history also has its successful failures, the two most notable being Abraham Lincoln and Winston Churchill. Both men rose to power in a crisis hour of their nation's history following a string of ignominious failures. And each in his own way became the greatest leader his nation has ever known. As Lincoln lay dying in a little rooming house across from Ford's Theatre where he was shot, a former detractor (Edwin Stanton) said, "There lies the most perfect ruler of men the world has ever seen...[and] now he belongs to the ages."[3]

It is not failure that makes or breaks a person, but how he responds to it. If he can learn from his failures, if he can persist in spite of failure, if he can maintain a positive attitude, a forward look, then he will succeed in life no matter how many times he may fail.

"After a long period of time in which Mr. Edison and his laboratory assistants had performed 699 experiments without finding what they were searching for, one assistant exclaimed in disgust, 'Six hundred and ninety-nine experiments and we have learned nothing.' Mr. Edison replied, 'Oh, yes, we have learned something. We have learned six hundred and ninety-nine things that will not work.' And, according to the report, on their seven hundredth effort they succeeded."[4]

"...though a righteous man falls seven times, he rises again...."[5]

ACTION STEPS:

☐ Compile your own list of successful "failures" — that is, men who failed before they succeeded. What can you learn from them? Be specific.

☐ How do you respond to failure in your own life? It may be helpful to recall a specific failure and to examine how you responded to it.

☐ Make a list of the changes you wish to make in the way you respond to failure. Be specific.

THOUGHT FOR THE DAY:

"Instead of accepting the fact that no one deserves the right to lead without first persevering through pain and heartache and failure, we resent those intruders. We treat them as enemies, not friends. We forget that the marks of greatness are not delivered in a paper sack by capricious gods. They are not hurriedly stuck onto skin like a tattoo.

"No, those who are really worth following have paid their dues. They have come through the furnace melted, beaten, reshaped, and tempered."[6]

— Charles R. Swindoll

PRAYER:

Lord, teach me to learn from my mistakes, to make peace with my pain, to see failure as a friend to guide me to success rather than a foe to destroy me. Give me the courage to get up and try again, no matter how many times I fail. In the name of Jesus I pray. Amen.

PROVERBS 25

1 *These are more proverbs of Solomon, copied by the men of Hezekiah king of Judah:*

2 *It is the glory of God to conceal a matter; to search out a matter is the glory of kings.*

3 *As the heavens are high and the earth is deep, so the hearts of kings are unsearchable.*

4 *Remove the dross from the silver, and out comes material for the silversmith;*

5 *remove the wicked from the king's presence, and his throne will be established through righteousness.*

6 *Do not exalt yourself in the king's presence, and do not claim a place among great men;*

7 *it is better for him to say to you, "Come up here," than for him to humiliate you before a nobleman. What you have seen with your eyes*

8 *do not bring hastily to court, for what will you do in the end if your neighbor puts you to shame?*

9 *If you argue your case with a neighbor, do not betray another man's confidence,*

10 *or he who hears it may shame you and you will never lose your bad reputation.*

11 *A word aptly spoken is like apples of gold in settings of silver.*

12 *Like an earring of gold or an ornament of fine gold is a wise man's rebuke to a listening ear.*

13 *Like the coolness of snow at harvest time is a trustworthy messenger to those who send him; he refreshes the spirit of his masters.*

14 *Like clouds and wind without rain is a man who boasts of gifts he does not give.*

15 *Through patience a ruler can be persuaded, and a gentle tongue can break a bone.*

16 *If you find honey, eat just enough — too much of it, and you will vomit.*

17 *Seldom set foot in your neighbor's house — too much of you, and he will hate you.*

PROVERBS 25

18 *Like a club or a sword or a sharp arrow is the man who gives false testimony against his neighbor.*

19 *Like a bad tooth or a lame foot is reliance on the unfaithful in times of trouble.*

20 *Like one who takes away a garment on a cold day, or like vinegar poured on soda, is one who sings songs to a heavy heart.*

21 *If your enemy is hungry, give him food to eat; if he is thirsty, give him water to drink.*

22 *In doing this, you will heap burning coals on his head, and the* LORD *will reward you.*

23 *As a north wind brings rain, so a sly tongue brings angry looks.*

24 *Better to live on a corner of the roof than share a house with a quarrelsome wife.*

25 *Like cold water to a weary soul is good news from a distant land.*

26 *Like a muddied spring or a polluted well is a righteous man who gives way to the wicked.*

27 *It is not good to eat too much honey, nor is it honorable to seek one's own honor.*

28 *Like a city whose walls are broken down is a man who lacks self-control.*

CHAPTER 25

TIMING IS EVERYTHING

Proverbs 25:1-28

Key verse: "Like one who takes away a garment on a cold day, or like vinegar poured on soda, is one who sings songs to a heavy heart."

— Proverbs 25:20

By nature, we men are problem solvers. It isn't something we have to think about, it just comes with the territory. Show us something that is broken, and we will try to fix it. Share a problem with us, and immediately we will try to solve it. While that masculine attribute equips us to function in the work place, it can be a painful liability in our marriage.

When a man's wife is hurting, when she's had a hard day or suffered an unsettling disappointment, the last thing she wants is his advise or a quick fix. Not realizing this, a man can get himself into some real hot water.

Take Bill for example. When Joyce arrives home after an exhausting day at the office and begins to share her frustrations, he listens just long enough to assess the situation before he starts offering solutions. When she tells him about a problem she is having with a co-worker, he has a ready answer. When she shares a concern she has about her relationship with her supervisor, he tells her that she worries too much. When she relates a problem one of the children is having with a classmate, he dismisses it as if it were nothing. "Don't get yourself all worked up," he says. "Let them work it out."

Finally, she gives up in exasperation and heads for the kitchen to begin dinner. Sensing her obvious frustration, he shouts after her, "Joyce, what are you upset about?" Slamming a cupboard door, she says, "Why can't you just listen to me?"

What we have here is a classic male/female misunderstanding. As a general rule, when a man shares a problem he is looking for a solution.

On the other hand, when a woman talks about her concerns she is simply looking for understanding. When he puts on his Mr. Fix-It hat and begins solving her problems, she feels that he is invalidating her feelings, which leaves her even more frustrated. When she continues to be upset after he has offered his solutions, it becomes increasingly difficult for him to listen because he feels useless, never realizing that all she wants is his empathy.

The real problem here is timing. A woman greatly appreciates her husband's problem-solving ability as long as he doesn't try to fix things when she's upset. At that time his advise is about as welcome as "...one who takes away a garment on a cold day...."[1] As Dr. John Gray points out in *Men Are from Mars, Women Are from Venus*, "Men need to remember that women talk about problems to get close and not necessarily to get solutions."[2]

ACTION STEPS:

☐ The next time your wife begins to share her problems, bite your tongue. Instead of offering advice, give her your shoulder to cry on. In time she will solve her own problems, and she will think you are the most understanding man in all the world.

☐ Make it a point to read *Men Are from Mars, Women Are from Venus* (HarperCollins) by John Gray, Ph.D., and discuss it with your wife.

THOUGHT FOR THE DAY:

"How had I missed this? She just needed me to go over and hold her. Another woman would have instinctively known what Bonnie needed. But as a man, I didn't know that touching, holding, and listening were so important to her. By recognizing these differences I began to learn a new way of relating to my wife."[3]

— John Gray, Ph.D.

PRAYER:

Lord, I like to be the hero, riding in on my white horse and solving all the problems. I've never stopped to realize that when I rescue my wife I make her feel like a helpless victim. Teach me to be more sensitive to her feelings and less concerned about my own. In the name of Jesus I pray. Amen.

PROVERBS 26

1 *Like snow in summer or rain in harvest, honor is not fitting for a fool.*

2 *Like a fluttering sparrow or a darting swallow, an undeserved curse does not come to rest.*

3 *A whip for the horse, a halter for the donkey, and a rod for the backs of fools!*

4 *Do not answer a fool according to his folly, or you will be like him yourself.*

5 *Answer a fool according to his folly, or he will be wise in his own eyes.*

6 *Like cutting off one's feet or drinking violence is the sending of a message by the hand of a fool.*

7 *Like a lame man's legs that hang limp is a proverb in the mouth of a fool.*

8 *Like tying a stone in a sling is the giving of honor to a fool.*

9 *Like a thornbush in a drunkard's hand is a proverb in the mouth of a fool.*

10 *Like an archer who wounds at random is he who hires a fool or any passer-by.*

11 *As a dog returns to its vomit, so a fool repeats his folly.*

12 *Do you see a man wise in his own eyes? There is more hope for a fool than for him.*

13 *The sluggard says, "There is a lion in the road, a fierce lion roaming the streets!"*

14 *As a door turns on its hinges, so a sluggard turns on his bed.*

15 *The sluggard buries his hand in the dish; he is too lazy to bring it back to his mouth.*

16 *The sluggard is wiser in his own eyes than seven men who answer discreetly.*

17 *Like one who seizes a dog by the ears is a passer-by who meddles in a quarrel not his own.*

18 *Like a madman shooting firebrands or deadly arrows*

19 *is a man who deceives his neighbor and says, "I was only joking!"*

20 *Without wood a fire goes out; without gossip a quarrel dies down.*

PROVERBS 26

21 *As charcoal to embers and as wood to fire, so is a quarrelsome man for kindling strife.*

22 *The words of a gossip are like choice morsels; they go down to a man's inmost parts.*

23 *Like a coating of glaze over earthenware are fervent lips with an evil heart.*

24 *A malicious man disguises himself with his lips, but in his heart he harbors deceit.*

25 *Though his speech is charming, do not believe him, for seven abominations fill his heart.*

26 *His malice may be concealed by deception, but his wickedness will be exposed in the assembly.*

27 *If a man digs a pit, he will fall into it; if a man rolls a stone, it will roll back on him.*

28 *A lying tongue hates those it hurts, and a flattering mouth works ruin.*

CHAPTER 26

RULES FOR HIRING

Proverbs 26:1-28

Key verse: "Like an archer who wounds at random is he who hires a fool or any passer-by."

— Proverbs 26:10

As I look back over nearly three decades of ministry, I realize that some of the best decisions I ever made were hiring decisions. By the same token, some of the worst decisions I ever made were also hiring decisions. The only comfort I can find is in the knowledge that I am not alone. When comparing notes with my ministerial colleagues, they readily acknowledge similar experiences. For the most part, our mistakes are painfully clear in retrospect, but at the time we were convinced that our decisions were good ones. Since the success of almost any endeavor depends upon the people we work with, let me share some of guidelines for hiring that I have learned through the years.

Rule #1: Don't hire a friend. Although some people can manage the difficult task of being both friend and boss, most of us can't. One of the first persons I called to serve on my staff was a close friend, and although he was enormously talented, it was an impossible situation. When I needed to give managerial direction, I ended up making friendly suggestions. When he should have deferred to my decisions as his boss, he appealed to our friendship. Finally, I was forced to ask for his resignation, and in the process I lost a dear friend.

Rule #2: Don't hire a primary leader to fill a supporting role. By temperament and talent some of us are primary leaders, and some of us are support personnel. When you try to squeeze a primary leader into a supporting role, you limit his effectiveness and increase his level of frustration. The narrow confines of his supporting role are like a cage, and he will constantly beat his wings against the bars. If you are not careful, he will challenge your role as primary leader, and even if you successfully withstand his challenge, the resulting fallout will have long-term consequences.

Rule #3: Don't plan on changing anyone after you hire him. After several frustrating experiences I have come to the conclusion that what you hire is what you get. You can train a person, but you can't change him. I know because I've tried it more times than I would like to remember.

One pastor tells of hiring a brilliant man: "His resume was impressive. Both his educational achievements and his work experience were exceptional. He was articulate, creative and possessed outstanding social skills."

Sounds great so far, doesn't it? Who among us wouldn't want a person like that on our staff? But wait, there's more.

"Too late," this pastor continues, "I discovered that he was also lazy. If I gave him an assignment he did it in record time, but that's as far as it went. He had little or no vision, no ideas of his own, and seemed intent on doing as little as possible."

I feel for that pastor because he's between a rock and a hard place. In a situation like that, he has only two choices — fire the man and deal with the consequences or live with him. Trying to change him is an absolute waste of time!

Rule #4: Check his references. Many hiring mistakes are made right here. If a man's resume looks good, and he has an impressive interview, it's tempting to bypass the tedious task of checking his references. Even if you know the applicant personally, you cannot afford to ignore this time-consuming task. What he is socially and what he is as an employee may not be anything alike. Only someone who has worked with him can give you the scoop on his work habits.

One final word of caution. Don't accept his references at face value. Consider their relationship to him and what they may stand to gain by giving him a positive recommendation. Carefully weigh their comments against your own "gut" feeling.

Rule #5: Remember, attitude is more important than either talent or experience. Most pastors I've talked with agree that nothing poisons staff relationships faster than a bad attitude. One smarting pastor referred to it as "staff infection," and he was only half kidding. Executives face the same thing with their management teams and readily admit that it is the bane of their jobs. Almost to a man they will tell you that there is not enough talent or experience to make up for a bad attitude. Nor is there any lack of experience or ineptitude that a great attitude cannot overcome.

A Princeton seminary professor made a study of great preachers in an attempt to discover the secret of their effectiveness: "He noted their tremendous varieties of personalities and gifts. Then he asked the question, 'What do these outstanding pulpiteers all have in common besides their faith?' After several years of searching he found the answer. It was their cheerfulness."[1] They had a positive attitude.

The same thing is true in the work place. A recent study by Telemetrics International determined that high achievers generally have a positive attitude, while low achievers usually have a poor attitude. As John Maxwell points out, "Usually the person who rises within an organization has a good attitude. The promotions did not give that individual an outstanding attitude, but an outstanding attitude resulted in promotions."[2]

ACTION STEPS:

☐ Although you may not be in a position where you are responsible for hiring people, the principles contained in this devotional may still speak to you. Ask yourself, "What is God saying to me through this material?"

☐ Are you now, or have you ever been, responsible for hiring people? If so, make a list of your hiring guidelines. How do they compare with the guidelines listed here?

☐ If you had one piece of advice to give on this matter, what would it be?

THOUGHT FOR THE DAY:

"A true and safe leader is likely to be one who has no desire to lead, but is forced into a position of leadership by the inward pressure of the Holy Spirit and the press of the external situation...I believe it might be accepted as a fairly reliable rule of thumb that the man who is ambitious to lead is disqualified as a leader."[3]

— A. W. Tozer

PRAYER:

Lord, when I think of some of the consequences of my hiring mistakes, I cringe. It wasn't just the principals involved who got hurt, but innocent bystanders as well. Heal the wounds my mistakes have caused and restore those who have fallen. In the future make me more sensitive to Your direction and less intent on having my own way. In the name of Jesus I pray. Amen.

PROVERBS 27

1 *Do not boast about tomorrow, for you do not know what a day may bring forth.*

2 *Let another praise you, and not your own mouth; someone else, and not your own lips.*

3 *Stone is heavy and sand a burden, but provocation by a fool is heavier than both.*

4 *Anger is cruel and fury overwhelming, but who can stand before jealousy?*

5 *Better is open rebuke than hidden love.*

6 *Wounds from a friend can be trusted, but an enemy multiplies kisses.*

7 *He who is full loathes honey, but to the hungry even what is bitter tastes sweet.*

8 *Like a bird that strays from its nest is a man who strays from his home.*

9 *Perfume and incense bring joy to the heart, and the pleasantness of one's friend springs from his earnest counsel.*

10 *Do not forsake your friend and the friend of your father, and do not go to your brother's house when disaster strikes you — better a neighbor nearby than a brother far away.*

11 *Be wise, my son, and bring joy to my heart; then I can answer anyone who treats me with contempt.*

12 *The prudent see danger and take refuge, but the simple keep going and suffer for it.*

13 *Take the garment of one who puts up security for a stranger; hold it in pledge if he does it for a wayward woman.*

14 *If a man loudly blesses his neighbor early in the morning, it will be taken as a curse.*

15 *A quarrelsome wife is like a constant dripping on a rainy day;*

16 *restraining her is like restraining the wind or grasping oil with the hand.*

17 *As iron sharpens iron, so one man sharpens another.*

18 *He who tends a fig tree will eat its fruit, and he who looks after his master will be honored.*

PROVERBS 27

19 *As water reflects a face, so a man's heart reflects the man.*

20 *Death and Destruction are never satisfied, and neither are the eyes of man.*

21 *The crucible for silver and the furnace for gold, but man is tested by the praise he receives.*

22 *Though you grind a fool in a mortar, grinding him like grain with a pestle, you will not remove his folly from him.*

23 *Be sure you know the condition of your flocks, give careful attention to your herds;*

24 *for riches do not endure forever, and a crown is not secure for all generations.*

25 *When the hay is removed and new growth appears and the grass from the hills is gathered in,*

26 *the lambs will provide you with clothing, and the goats with the price of a field.*

27 *You will have plenty of goats' milk to feed you and your family and to nourish your servant girls.*

CHAPTER 27

THE DANGERS OF SUCCESS

Proverbs 27:1-27

Key verse: "The crucible for silver and the furnace for gold, but man is tested by the praise he receives."

— Proverbs 27:21

If you really want to know what a man is made of, put him under pressure. Let him experience either adversity or success.

Given a choice, most of us would probably choose to be tested by success even though we realize that it is far harder to handle. As Thomas Carlyle, the Scottish essayist and historian, noted, "...for one man who can stand prosperity, there are a hundred that will stand adversity."[1]

Adversity tests a man's character, his ability to hang in there when the going gets tough. Success, on the other hand, tests a man's integrity, his ability to remain true to himself, to remain morally and ethically pure.

"When adversity strikes," as Chuck Swindoll points out, "life becomes rather simple. Our need is to survive. But when prosperity occurs, life gets complicated. And our needs are numerous, often extremely complex. Invariably, our integrity is put to the test."[2]

This is what the wise man is talking about when he writes, "The crucible for silver and the furnace for gold, but man is tested by the praise he receives."[3]

Let's consider for a moment what makes success so dangerous. First, it tends to produce pride. It leads a man to believe that he has succeeded through his own efforts and ingenuity, to believe that he is a self-made man.

Nothing could be further from the truth. Every talent and ability that any of us has comes from God. We can no more take credit for our gifts than a man seven feet tall can take credit for his height. Nor can we take credit for our success, because the Scriptures say, "No one from the east or the west or from the desert can exalt a man. But it is God who judges: He brings one down, he exalts another."[4]

The second thing that makes success so difficult to handle is that it exposes a man to temptations he has never before had to face. Suddenly he has more disposable income than he knows what to do with. He is invited to serve on prestigious boards and committees. Important people seek his advice. He now moves in circles where anything he wants can be had for a price. Powerful people court him, take him into their confidence, put him in their debt. Tragically, many a man discovers that his goodness has come not from a pure heart, but only from lack of an opportunity to do evil.

Those who pass the test of praise usually do so because they refuse to take themselves or their achievements too seriously. They see success not as a plum to be picked, but as a responsibility to be fulfilled toward God and their fellow man. Like Daniel of old, they are "...neither corrupt nor negligent."[5] And even their enemies are forced to conclude: "...'We will never find any basis for charges against this man....'"[6]

ACTION STEPS:

☐ Both Joseph and Daniel were men who remained faithful not only in adversity, but also when exalted to positions of great power. Read their stories in Genesis Chapters 37-50 and Daniel Chapters 1-12 and see if you can identify the character traits that enabled them to remain true to their convictions.

☐ Examine yourself: Are those same character traits present in your own life? Please explain.

☐ Ask yourself what you can do to prepare yourself for the test of praise. Be specific.

THOUGHT FOR THE DAY:

"No man can give at once the impressions that he himself is clever and that Christ is mighty to save. If a person does not subdue this craving for attention and recognition, he will fall utterly short of the goal for which he was designed."[7]

— James Denney

PRAYER:

Lord, prepare me for whatever the future may bring. Give me the gift of contentment that I may labor in obscurity, if that is what You should choose. Give me genuine humility that I may handle success, if that is what You should choose. In the name of Jesus, I pray. Amen.

PROVERBS 28

1 *The wicked man flees though no one pursues, but the righteous are as bold as a lion.*

2 *When a country is rebellious, it has many rulers, but a man of understanding and knowledge maintains order.*

3 *A ruler who oppresses the poor is like a driving rain that leaves no crops.*

4 *Those who forsake the law praise the wicked, but those who keep the law resist them.*

5 *Evil men do not understand justice, but those who seek the* LORD *understand it fully.*

6 *Better a poor man whose walk is blameless than a rich man whose ways are perverse.*

7 *He who keeps the law is a discerning son, but a companion of gluttons disgraces his father.*

8 *He who increases his wealth by exorbitant interest amasses it for another, who will be kind to the poor.*

9 *If anyone turns a deaf ear to the law, even his prayers are detestable.*

10 *He who leads the upright along an evil path will fall into his own trap, but the blameless will receive a good inheritance.*

11 *A rich man may be wise in his own eyes, but a poor man who has discernment sees through him.*

12 *When the righteous triumph, there is great elation; but when the wicked rise to power, men go into hiding.*

13 *He who conceals his sins does not prosper, but whoever confesses and renounces them finds mercy.*

14 *Blessed is the man who always fears the* LORD, *but he who hardens his heart falls into trouble.*

15 *Like a roaring lion or a charging bear is a wicked man ruling over a helpless people.*

16 *A tyrannical ruler lacks judgment, but he who hates ill-gotten gain will enjoy a long life.*

17 *A man tormented by the guilt of murder will be a fugitive till death; let no one support him.*

PROVERBS 28

18 *He whose walk is blameless is kept safe, but he whose ways are*
perverse will suddenly fall.
19 *He who works his land will have abundant food, but the one who*
chases fantasies will have his fill of poverty.
20 *A faithful man will be richly blessed, but one eager to get rich will*
not go unpunished.
21 *To show partiality is not good — yet a man will do wrong for a*
piece of bread.
22 *A stingy man is eager to get rich and is unaware that poverty*
awaits him.
23 *He who rebukes a man will in the end gain more favor than he*
who has a flattering tongue.
24 *He who robs his father or mother and says, "It's not wrong"— he*
is partner to him who destroys.
25 *A greedy man stirs up dissension, but he who trusts in the* LORD
will prosper.
26 *He who trusts in himself is a fool, but he who walks in wisdom is*
kept safe.
27 *He who gives to the poor will lack nothing, but he who closes his*
eyes to them receives many curses.
28 *When the wicked rise to power, people go into hiding; but when the*
wicked perish, the righteous thrive.

CHAPTER 28

DEADLY SECRETS AND HEALING GRACE

Proverbs 28:1-28

Key verse: "He who conceals his sins does not prosper, but whoever confesses and renounces them finds mercy."

— Proverbs 28:13

In his book *Rebuilding Your Broken World*, Gordon MacDonald writes, "Studies suggest that more than half of American mid-life males live with at least one secret in the past of their personal lives, and these men believe its revelation would bring about catastrophic consequences for them and those close to them."[1]

If this is true, and my personal experience as a pastor and counselor seems to verify it, then there are a lot of hurting men out there.

Initially, a man's secret sin will be a source of deep distress. Hear King David as he describes the inner turmoil he experienced the year he tried to keep secret his adulterous affair with Bathsheba. "When I kept silent," he says, "my bones wasted away through my groaning all day long. For day and night your [God's] hand was heavy upon me; my strength was sapped as in the heat of summer."[2]

And again he confesses, "My guilt has overwhelmed me like a burden too heavy to bear...I am bowed down and brought very low; all day long I go about mourning. My back is filled with searing pain; there is no health in my body. I am feeble and utterly crushed; I groan in anguish of heart."[3]

If you are living in secret sin, you know what David is talking about. Your heart hurts. You despise yourself. Shame has made you sick, and you have little or no energy. Weariness weights you down, but sleep won't come. Fear eats at your belly. Depression dogs your days. You feel trapped and are tempted to run away, but where can you go to escape yourself? Thoughts of suicide entice you with promises of sweet oblivion, but fear of the eternal consequences stay your hand.

There is only one way to put an end to your torment, only one way to escape your prison of pain. Confess your sins and renounce them, come clean with God.

Although it is true that only God can forgive sin, I am convinced that secret sin can only be overcome by confessing it to another person. Sin flourishes in the dark, it thrives in secret; but expose it to the light by honest confession to a fellow believer, and it withers and dies.

Let me offer a word of advice here. Choose your confessor carefully. He should be a mature believer, a man of integrity, trustworthy, compassionate and nonjudgmental.

Not infrequently, I am asked by husbands guilty of sexual sin if they should tell their wives. While each situation must be considered on its own merits, as a general rule I think not. If a man's wife has absolutely no idea of his philandering, then he should think long and hard before he tells her. Why make her suffer for his sins? On the other hand, if she questions him, he must tell her the absolute truth. He must not lie to her.

God is longsuffering and merciful. More than anything, He wants to deliver you from your sinful trap. If you will voluntarily confess your sins and renounce them, God has no desire to make them public. However, if you persist in your clandestine ways, He has no choice but to expose your sins. Even then His intent is mercy rather than judgment. Above all, He wants to forgive your sins and deliver you from your self-made hell!

When Nathan the prophet finally confronted King David about his sinful affair with Bathsheba, it was both painfully humbling and wonderfully liberating. It was humbling in the sense that David's sin was made public knowledge. He could no longer pretend to be something he was not. It was liberating because he could stop pretending and throw himself on the mercies of God.

Hear David as he worships the Lord and celebrates his deliverance: "Then I acknowledged my sin to you and did not cover up my iniquity. I said, 'I will confess my transgressions to the Lord' — and you forgave the guilt of my sin."[4]

His sorrow has now been turned into joy and he shouts aloud the praises of God his Savior. "Blessed is he whose transgressions are forgiven, whose sins are covered. Blessed is the man whose sin the Lord does not count against him and in whose spirit is no deceit."[5]

Be assured that your sins will find you out. The only choice you have is in regard to how.

To my knowledge there is no scriptural reason why your transgression need be made public if you have forsaken your sin, voluntarily confessed it and made yourself accountable to a mature brother. On the other hand, if you persist in continuing your double life, then God has no choice but to allow your sin to become common knowledge in hopes of bringing you to repentance.

Remember, "He who conceals his sins does not prosper, but whoever confesses and renounces them finds mercy."[6]

ACTION STEPS:

☐ If there is secret sin in your life, confess it to God right now and receive His forgiveness.

☐ Make yourself accountable to your pastor or a trusted Christian brother. Confess your secret sin to him.

☐ Make whatever changes are necessary to cut off all contact with the persons and places where your secret sin flourished.

THOUGHT FOR THE DAY:

"I thought of what might be called the underside of the church: those numberless people who walk into sanctuaries all over the world carrying their secrets behind bright clothing and forced smiles. They sing the songs, pray the prayers, listen to the sermons. And all the while the secrets fester within the private world causing either a constantly broken heart or a hardened heart. They come in fear of their secrets being exposed, and they quite likely go in fear that they will have to live this way for the rest of their lives. Believe me, the underside of the church is there, listening and watching to find out whether there is anyone with whom their secret might be safe if revealed."[7]

— Gordon MacDonald

PRAYER:

Lord, I confess my secret sin. I name it. I have no excuses, no self-justifying rationalizations. It was my fault. I am to blame. Forgive me, I pray, and change me. Make me truly Your person in both thought and deed. In the name of Jesus I pray. Amen.

PROVERBS 29

1 *A man who remains stiff-necked after many rebukes will suddenly be destroyed—without remedy.*

2 *When the righteous thrive, the people rejoice; when the wicked rule, the people groan.*

3 *A man who loves wisdom brings joy to his father, but a companion of prostitutes squanders his wealth.*

4 *By justice a king gives a country stability, but one who is greedy for bribes tears it down.*

5 *Whoever flatters his neighbor is spreading a net for his feet.*

6 *An evil man is snared by his own sin, but a righteous one can sing and be glad.*

7 *The righteous care about justice for the poor, but the wicked have no such concern.*

8 *Mockers stir up a city, but wise men turn away anger.*

9 *If a wise man goes to court with a fool, the fool rages and scoffs, and there is no peace.*

10 *Bloodthirsty men hate a man of integrity and seek to kill the upright.*

11 *A fool gives full vent to his anger, but a wise man keeps himself under control.*

12 *If a ruler listens to lies, all his officials become wicked.*

13 *The poor man and the oppressor have this in common: The* LORD *gives sight to the eyes of both.*

14 *If a king judges the poor with fairness, his throne will always be secure.*

15 *The rod of correction imparts wisdom, but a child left to himself disgraces his mother.*

16 *When the wicked thrive, so does sin, but the righteous will see their downfall.*

17 *Discipline your son, and he will give you peace; he will bring delight to your soul.*

18 *Where there is no revelation, the people cast off restraint; but blessed is he who keeps the law.*

19 *A servant cannot be corrected by mere words; though he understands, he will not respond.*

PROVERBS 29

20 *Do you see a man who speaks in haste? There is more hope for a fool than for him.*

21 *If a man pampers his servant from youth, he will bring grief in the end.*

22 *An angry man stirs up dissension, and a hot-tempered one commits many sins.*

23 *A man's pride brings him low, but a man of lowly spirit gains honor.*

24 *The accomplice of a thief is his own enemy; he is put under oath and dare not testify.*

25 *Fear of man will prove to be a snare, but whoever trusts in the* LORD *is kept safe.*

26 *Many seek an audience with a ruler, but it is from the* LORD *that man gets justice.*

27 *The righteous detest the dishonest; the wicked detest the upright.*

CHAPTER 29

THE COURAGE TO DO WHAT'S RIGHT

Proverbs 29:1-27
Key verse: "Fear of man will prove to be a snare, but whoever trusts in the Lord is kept safe."
— Proverbs 29:25

It was July 1991, and I was in Wichita, Kansas, attending a pro-life rally as part of the "Summer of Mercy." I don't remember who the speaker was or anything that he said, but I have never been able to forget what happened to me at the end of that service. The leaders of Operation Rescue asked for volunteers to risk arrest by non-violently blocking the entrance to an abortion clinic in a peaceful attempt to prevent mothers from having the children in their wombs put to death.

As the call was issued, my heart began a slow, heavy beating. Time seemed to stand still, and it felt as if I stood alone in the presence of God. With undeniable clarity I heard Him ask, "Will you go?" It wasn't an audible voice, not one I could hear with my ear, but a knowing in my spirit. God was asking me to risk the disapproval of men in obedience to Him.

In that moment I found myself face to face with fear. I wasn't so much afraid of being arrested, though I have the utmost respect for the law and those who enforce it. Nor was I really afraid of the disapproval of my peers and others who might misunderstand what I was doing. No, I feared that I might waste my life, might throw it away on a hopeless cause.

I found myself arguing with God, telling Him that I would willingly sacrifice my life, that I would gladly die, if I could be assured that by doing so no more babies would die at the hands of the abortionists. In that moment I truly meant it. I would have gladly exchanged my life for the lives of millions of unborn babies. What I wasn't willing to do was to throw my life away for no good reason. What if I was arrested and spent months or even years in jail, and nothing changed? That was a risk I simply wasn't ready to take.

Again God spoke to me, clearly, distinctly, in my spirit. This time He said, "Nothing you do in obedience to Me is ever wasted, no matter how it may appear at the time." To this day His words resonate in my spirit, and they have become the heart of my commitment — "Nothing you do in obedience to Me is ever wasted...."

Although you may never find yourself trying to decide if you should "rescue" or not, you will be confronted with innumerable opportunities to compromise your faith rather than risk the disapproval of men. In those moments you will have to decide whether you are going to fear and obey God, or man.

In small ways, and sometimes not so small ways, we confront this issue every day in the work place. Will I compromise my convictions in order to be accepted as one of the guys? Will I look the other way while some unethical things are done in order to close the deal? Will I do the right thing, no matter what the cost, or will I play along rather than risk rocking the boat?

No one has ever handled this challenge more effectively than Daniel. As a young man he was taken captive by the Babylonians and transported from his native Jerusalem to Babylon. He was inducted into the service of King Nebuchadnezzar and subjected to three years of intense brainwashing. He was taught both the language and the literature of the Babylonians. Furthermore, he was commanded to eat food and wine from the king's table. At this point "...Daniel resolved not to defile himself with the royal food and wine...."[1]

It has been suggested that what "Daniel perceived (correctly) in this food allotment was an effort to seduce him into the lifestyle of a Babylonian through the enjoyment of pleasures he had never before known...No mention is made of Daniel being confronted with an apologetic for Babylonian theology or with intellectual arguments against Old Testament faith. The attack was far more subtle than that, and therefore potentially far more lethal. Somebody in Nebuchadnezzar's palace knew enough about the human heart to see that most men have their price, and that good times, comfort, self-esteem, and a position in society are usually a sufficient bid for a soul."[2]

In many ways Daniel's future greatness depended on that single decision. Had he compromised there, he would never have found himself in the positions he later occupied nor would he have been faithful enough to cope with them as he did. "Instead, from the beginning, in what to others seemed a trivial matter, he nailed his colors to the mast. In doing so, he gained a bridgehead into enemy-occupied territory and found himself increasingly strong in the Lord."[3]

It is as true today as it was in Daniel's day: "Fear of man will prove to be a snare, but whoever trusts in the Lord is kept safe."[4]

ACTION STEPS:

☐ Think of a time when you had to choose between pleasing men or pleasing God. What did you do? Why?

☐ Have you ever made a decision based on the fear of what others would think? Please explain. Solomon says, "Fear of man will prove to be a snare...."[5] Can you see how your decision to please others led to a trap? Please explain.

☐ Right now ask God to give you the wisdom and the courage to always do the right thing, no matter what the cost.

THOUGHT FOR THE DAY:

"Give me a hundred men who fear nothing but sin, and desire nothing but God, and I will shake the world. I care not a straw whether they be clergymen or laymen; and such alone will overthrow the kingdom of Satan and build up the Kingdom of God on earth."[6]

— John Wesley

PRAYER:

Lord, give me the courage to do the right thing, no matter how much I fear the consequences. In the name of Jesus I pray. Amen.

PROVERBS 30

1 *The sayings of Agur son of Jakeh—an oracle: This man declared to Ithiel, to Ithiel and to Ucal:*

2 *I am the most ignorant of men; I do not have a man's understanding.*

3 *I have not learned wisdom, nor have I knowledge of the Holy One.*

4 *Who has gone up to heaven and come down? Who has gathered up the wind in the hollow of his hands? Who has wrapped up the waters in his cloak? Who has established all the ends of the earth? What is his name, and the name of his son? Tell me if you know!*

5 *Every word of God is flawless; he is a shield to those who take refuge in him.*

6 *Do not add to his words, or he will rebuke you and prove you a liar.*

7 *Two things I ask of you,* O LORD; *do not refuse me before I die:*

8 *Keep falsehood and lies far from me; give me neither poverty nor riches, but give me only my daily bread.*

9 *Otherwise, I may have too much and disown you and say, "Who is the* LORD*?" Or I may become poor and steal, and so dishonor the name of my God.*

10 *Do not slander a servant to his master, or he will curse you, and you will pay for it.*

11 *There are those who curse their fathers and do not bless their mothers;*

12 *those who are pure in their own eyes and yet are not cleansed of their filth;*

13 *those whose eyes are ever so haughty, whose glances are so disdainful;*

14 *those whose teeth are swords and whose jaws are set with knives to devour the poor from the earth, the needy from among mankind.*

15 *The leech has two daughters. "Give! Give!" they cry. "There are three things that are never satisfied, four that never say, "Enough!":*

16 *the grave, the barren womb, land, which is never satisfied with water, and fire, which never says, "Enough!"*

17 *The eye that mocks a father, that scorns obedience to a mother, will be pecked out by the ravens of the valley, will be eaten by the vultures.*

PROVERBS 30

18 *There are three things that are too amazing for me, four that I do not understand:*
19 *the way of an eagle in the sky, the way of a snake on a rock, the way of a ship on the high seas, and the way of a man with a maiden.*
20 *This is the way of an adulteress: She eats and wipes her mouth and says, "I've done nothing wrong."*
21 *Under three things the earth trembles, under four it cannot bear up:*
22 *a servant who becomes king, a fool who is full of food,*
23 *an unloved woman who is married, and a maidservant who displaces her mistress.*
24 *Four things on earth are small, yet they are extremely wise:*
25 *Ants are creatures of little strength, yet they store up their food in the summer;*
26 *coneys are creatures of little power, yet they make their home in the crags;*
27 *locusts have no king, yet they advance together in ranks;*
28 *a lizard can be caught with the hand, yet it is found in kings' palaces.*
29 *There are three things that are stately in their stride, four that move with stately bearing:*
30 *a lion, mighty among beasts, who retreats before nothing;*
31 *a strutting rooster, a he-goat, and a king with his army around him.*
32 *If you have played the fool and exalted yourself, or if you have planned evil, clap your hand over your mouth!*
33 *For as churning the milk produces butter, and as twisting the nose produces blood, so stirring up anger produces strife.*

CHAPTER 30

EVERY PROMISE IN THE BOOK

Proverbs 30:1-33

Key verse: "Every word of God is flawless;
he is a shield to those who take refuge in him."
— Proverbs 30:5

While I was kneeling in prayer, the reference Isaiah 41:9 sprang into my mind as clearly as any thought I have ever had. With an effort I dismissed it and returned to my prayers. Almost immediately it returned, and once more I thrust it from my mind. By concentrating I was able to focus on my prayers, but if I relaxed my stern self-control for even a moment, the thought returned, clearer and more insistent than ever.

Belatedly, I decided that God might be trying to tell me something so I found my Bible and opened it to Isaiah 41. Beginning at verse nine I read, "'..."You are my servant"; I have chosen you and have not rejected you. So do not fear, for I am with you; do not be dismayed, for I am your God. I will strengthen you and help you; I will uphold you with my righteous right hand. All who rage against you will surely be ashamed and disgraced; those who oppose you will be as nothing and perish. Though you search for your enemies, you will not find them. Those who wage war against you will be as nothing at all. For I am the Lord, your God, who takes hold of your right hand and says to you, Do not fear; I will help you.'"[1]

At the time I found the passage encouraging, but hardly earth-shattering. I promptly forgot it, never realizing that in a few weeks I would be clinging to it for dear life. In fact, in the dark days ahead it would become my hope, my source of strength.

Here's what happened. With absolutely no warning, I was publicly dismissed from my position as associate pastor. That was bad enough in and of itself, but it was just the latest in a continuing series of crises in our lives. Just weeks earlier we had cut our vacation short and rushed home to be with Brenda's mother as she underwent surgery to remove a grapefruit-sized tumor. Of course, we feared the worst, and although no one uttered the "C" word, it hung over us like a cloud. When the doctors informed us that the surgery was successful and the tumor was not malignant, we experienced euphoric relief. Imagine our dismay when two days later they told us that her ovaries were cancerous.

With God's help we fought our way through the frightening possibilities that raised and tried to prepare ourselves for the trauma of radiation therapy. Now, on top of everything else, I was unemployed and without any immediate prospects of rectifying our uncertain situation. Still, as I told Brenda, we had nine years' experience in the ministry, and I figured it was just a matter of time before we were called to a new church.

While Brenda concentrated on homemaking and taking care of our daughter Leah, I begin sending out resumes. Before long I had more than thirty in the mail, and I was sure we would receive a call to a new congregation any day. Unfortunately, the weeks stretched into months without a single positive response, and my earlier optimism gave way to bouts of depression. I even had days when I seriously doubted that there was any place for me in the ministry.

Sometimes I would lie awake in the dead of night wondering what the future held. Brenda's mother was deathly ill from the radiation treatments, and I seriously doubted if she was going to make it. Statistically, she didn't seem to have much of a chance. Ovarian cancer is fatal 95 percent of the time. I didn't tell Brenda any of this, but I could tell she was fighting fears of her own.

As our situation grew more desperate, my depression deepened. In anger I railed at God. Why had He abandoned us? Why didn't He answer our prayers? Why didn't He intervene in our behalf? Well do I remember telling Him that He wasn't much of a Father, that I was just a man, but I would never treat my daughter the way He was treating us.

Somewhere in the midst of that tirade I suddenly remembered Isaiah 41. With trembling hands I opened my Bible and turned to Isaiah. Finding the forty-first chapter, I begin to read. Through tear-blurred eyes I made out the words — God's word to me, to us! "...'do not fear, for I am with you; do not be dismayed, for I am your God....those who oppose you will be as nothing and perish. Though you search for your enemies, you will not find them....'"[2]

Then it hit me. Months ago, before I had really had any idea that I would need a word from the Lord, God had given me this passage. Before I had even known enough to ask, God had already answered my prayer.[3] Armed with the flawless promise of the Father, I now faced the future with renewed hope. I had nothing to fear, for God was my shield.

Our circumstances did not change immediately, but our attitude did. In time we were invited to become pastors of the Church of the Comforter in Craig, Colorado, where we served for more than five years. From there we went to Christian Chapel in Tulsa, Oklahoma, where we enjoyed more than twelve years of fruitful ministry. And best of all, Brenda's mother beat the odds. It has now been nearly twenty years since she completed her radiation treatments, and the doctors have never been able to find another trace of cancer in her body.

Well did God say it: "Though you search for your enemies, you will not find them. Those who wage war against you will be as nothing at all. For I am the Lord, your God, who takes hold of your right hand and says to you, Do not fear; I will help you."[4]

ACTION STEPS:

☐ Can you remember a time when God made some passage of Scripture especially alive for you? Go back and reread that passage and spend a few minutes reliving that experience.

☐ Make a list of some of your favorite Scriptures, the ones that have been particularly helpful to you across the years.

☐ Make it a point to share at least one of your Scriptures with your wife or a brother in the Lord. Invite them to share one of their favorite passages as well.

THOUGHT FOR THE DAY:

"Do not let it be imagined that one must remain silent about one's feelings of rebellion in order to enter into dialogue with God. Quite the opposite is the truth: it is precisely when one expresses them that a dialogue of truth begins...By giving expression to his reproaches he becomes more sincere — and the dialogue can begin."[5]

— Paul Tournier

PRAYER:

Lord, You are my refuge and my strength, a very present help in time of trouble. I thank You for Your Word which has guided and sustained me in the dark hours when it seemed my faith would fail. May I continue to hide it in my heart against the difficult days ahead. In the name of Jesus I pray. Amen.

PROVERBS 31

1 *The sayings of King Lemuel—an oracle his mother taught him:*

2 *O my son, O son of my womb, O son of my vows,*

3 *do not spend your strength on women, your vigor on those who ruin kings.*

4 *It is not for kings, O Lemuel — not for kings to drink wine, not for rulers to crave beer,*

5 *lest they drink and forget what the law decrees, and deprive all the oppressed of their rights.*

6 *Give beer to those who are perishing, wine to those who are in anguish;*

7 *let them drink and forget their poverty and remember their misery no more.*

8 *Speak up for those who cannot speak for themselves, for the rights of all who are destitute.*

9 *Speak up and judge fairly; defend the rights of the poor and needy.*

10 *A wife of noble character who can find? She is worth far more than rubies.*

11 *Her husband has full confidence in her and lacks nothing of value.*

12 *She brings him good, not harm, all the days of her life.*

13 *She selects wool and flax and works with eager hands.*

14 *She is like the merchant ships, bringing her food from afar.*

15 *She gets up while it is still dark; she provides food for her family and portions for her servant girls.*

16 *She considers a field and buys it; out of her earnings she plants a vineyard.*

17 *She sets about her work vigorously; her arms are strong for her tasks.*

18 *She sees that her trading is profitable, and her lamp does not go out at night.*

19 *In her hand she holds the distaff and grasps the spindle with her fingers.*

20 *She opens her arms to the poor and extends her hands to the needy.*

21 *When it snows, she has no fear for her household; for all of them are clothed in scarlet.*

PROVERBS 31

22 *She makes coverings for her bed; she is clothed in fine linen and purple.*

23 *Her husband is respected at the city gate, where he takes his seat among the elders of the land.*

24 *She makes linen garments and sells them, and supplies the merchants with sashes.*

25 *She is clothed with strength and dignity; she can laugh at the days to come.*

26 *She speaks with wisdom, and faithful instruction is on her tongue.*

27 *She watches over the affairs of her household and does not eat the bread of idleness.*

28 *Her children arise and call her blessed; her husband also, and he praises her:*

29 *"Many women do noble things, but you surpass them all."*

30 *Charm is deceptive, and beauty is fleeting; but a woman who fears the* LORD *is to be praised.*

31 *Give her the reward she has earned, and let her works bring her praise at the city gate.*

CHAPTER 31

A GIFT FROM GOD

Proverbs 31:1-31

Key verses: "A wife of noble character who can find? She is worth far more than rubies. Her husband has full confidence in her and lacks nothing of value...Charm is deceptive, and beauty is fleeting; but a woman who fears the Lord is to be praised."

— Proverbs 31:10,11,30

Throughout this book we have talked of many things, but we have saved the best till last — a wife of noble character. Of all of God's gifts, none — other than the gift of His dear Son — is so precious. Well did Solomon say, "Houses and wealth are inherited from parents, but a prudent wife is from the Lord."[1]

Now I know there are some thoughtless, narcissistic guys out there, and if you happen to be one of them this chapter will be a bit much for you. They are the kind of husbands who think of no one but themselves. As far as they are concerned, Proverbs 31 is just a measuring stick to intimidate their wife or a club with which to beat her.

Wrong!

Proverbs 31 is a wise husband's tribute to his wife, and as such it begs to be read as a way of reminding us of all the selfless things our wives do to make our house a home. Space does not permit me to mention them all, but let me remind you of four or five. If you catch sight of your wife in the wise man's portrait, make it a point to tell her.

First, a wife of noble character is selfless. "She gets up while it is still dark; she provides food for her family...She sets about her work vigorously...her lamp does not go out at night."[2]

Who's the first to arise in the morning? She is, and while we and the children are still tucked snugly in your beds, she is preparing breakfast and making lunches. Who's the last to retire for the night? She is. While we lie in bed reading a few pages of a favorite book, she looks in on the children one last time, makes sure the house is straight and checks the thermostat. No one is more conscientious than she.

Second, a wife of noble character is wise in her counsel. "She speaks with wisdom, and faithful instruction is on her tongue."[3] Well do I remember the wise counsel Brenda has given me through the years. And with chagrin do I remember the times I ignored it to my own detriment. Even then she had the grace not to say, "I told you so."

Third, a wife of noble character sees that her family is well clothed. "When it snows, she has no fear for her household; for all of them are clothed in scarlet."[4]

When Leah was growing up, Brenda spent countless hours at the sewing machine making her beautiful clothes for every occasion, and each seam was stitched with love. How pretty Leah looked dressed in her mother's handiwork, and how beloved. Still today Brenda looks to the needs of her family. Only God knows how many hours she spends searching the malls for the perfect sweater or tie. Only the best will do for the man in her life. Thanks, Brenda, for making me look better than I have any right to.

Fourth, a wife of noble character has a great sense of humor. "She is clothed with strength and dignity; she can laugh at the days to come."[5] Blessed is the man who is married to a woman who can take a joke. And doubly blessed is he if she can give as good as she gets. Never will I forget the time I started caressing Brenda in the middle of the night. While pretending to be asleep she mumbled, "Stop it. You're just like Richard!" Needless to say, that stopped me in my tracks, and Brenda laughed until she cried.

Fifth, a wife of noble character has a compassionate heart. "She opens her arms to the poor and extends her hands to the needy."[6] As a pastor, many was the time I brought some homeless family home for dinner or to spend the night. Without a word of complaint, Brenda set extra places at the table or made pallets on the floor. Whether it was a grieving child, a battered wife or just some guy down on his luck, Brenda could always find room for them in the parsonage.

The wise man says, "Charm is deceptive, and beauty is fleeting; but a woman who fears the Lord is to be praised. Give her the reward she has earned, and let her works bring her praise at the city gate...Her children arise and call her blessed; her husband also, and he praises her."[7]

ACTION STEPS:

☐ Make a list of the things you most appreciate about your wife. Now take her out to a nice restaurant. After dinner take a few minutes to share your list with her.

☐ Sit down with the children and help them make a list of all the nice things their mother does for them. Find an appropriate time when they can share their list with her.

THOUGHT FOR THE DAY:

"He who finds a wife finds what is good and receives favor from the Lord."[8]

— Solomon

PRAYER:

Lord, I thank You for the gift of my wife. When I grow weary, she strengthens me. When disappointment or failure tempts me to lose heart, she encourages me. When I'm not the man I should be, she forgives me. And when I achieve some small success, she celebrates as if it were her own. Truly, her love is the light of my life. In the name of Jesus I pray. Amen.

WHAT IS YOUR DECISION?

If you have never received Jesus Christ as your personal Lord and Savior, why not do it right now? Simply repeat this prayer with sincerity: "Lord Jesus, I believe that You are the Son of God. I believe that You became man and died on the cross for my sins. I believe that God raised you from the dead and made You the Savior of the world. I confess that I am a sinner and I ask You to forgive me, and to cleanse me of all my sins. I accept Your forgiveness, and I receive You as my Lord and Savior. In Jesus' name, I pray. Amen."

"...if you confess with your mouth, 'Jesus is Lord,' and believe in your heart that God raised him from the dead, you will be saved. For it is with your heart that you believe and are justified, and it is with your mouth that you confess and are saved...for, 'Everyone who calls on the name of the Lord will be saved.'"

Romans 10:9,10,13

"If we confess our sins, he is faithful and just and will forgive us our sins and purify us from all unrighteousness."

1 John 1:9

Now that you have accepted Jesus as your Savior:

1. Read your Bible *daily* — it is your spiritual food that will make you a strong Christian.
2. Pray and talk to God daily — He desires for the two of you to communicate and share your lives with each other.
3. Share your faith with others. Be bold to let others know that Jesus loves them.
4. Regularly attend a local church where Jesus is preached, where you can serve Him and where you can fellowship with other believers.
5. Let His love in your heart touch the lives of others by your good works done in His name.

Please let us know of the decision you made. Write:

Honor Books
P.O. 55388
Tulsa, OK 74155

ENDNOTES

CHAPTER 1

[1]Exodus 15:11; Psalm 99:9; Isaiah 6:1-3; Revelation 4:8.

[2]Deuteronomy 32:4; Jeremiah 9:23,24; Revelation 15:3.

[3]Psalm 97:1,2; Psalm 119:137; Jeremiah 23:6.

[4]Exodus 20:19.

[5]Jeremiah 31:3; John 3:16; Romans 5:8.

[6]Ephesians 2:4; James 5:11; 1 Peter 1:3.

[7]Ephesians 2:8; Hebrews 4:16; 1 Peter 5:10.

[8]Hebrews 2:14-18; Hebrews 4:15,16.

[9]Isaiah 53:4,10,12.

[10]Romans 5:8.

[11]David A. Hubbard, *The Communicator's Commentary Series, Old Testament, Volume 15A: Proverbs* (Dallas: Word Books Publisher, 1989), p. 48.

CHAPTER 2

[1]James 1:5.

[2]Proverbs 11:15.

[3]Proverbs 6:10,11.

[4]Proverbs 13:3.

[5]Proverbs 11:24,25.

[6]Proverbs 13:11.

[7]Proverbs 13:20.

[8]Matthew 6:33.

[9]Matthew 10:39.

[10]2 Chronicles 1:10.

[11]M. Basil Pennington, *Centering Prayer*, quoted in *Disciplines for the Inner Life* by Bob Benson and Michael W. Benson (Waco: Word Books Publisher, 1985), p. 164.

CHAPTER 3

[1]Proverbs 3:5.

[2]Proverbs 3:6 TLB.

[3]Michel Quoist, *Prayers* (Kansas City: Sheed and Ward, 1963), pp. 120,123.

CHAPTER 4

[1]Matthew 12:35 KJV.

[2]Proverbs 4:23.

[3]Gordon MacDonald, *Rebuilding Your Broken World* (Nashville: Oliver-Nelson Books, a division of Thomas Nelson, Inc., Publishers, 1988), p. 30.

[4]Oswald Chambers, *The Place of Help*, quoted in *Rebuilding Your Broken World* by Gordon MacDonald (Nashville: Oliver-Nelson Books, a division of Thomas Nelson, Inc., Publishers, 1988), p. 54.

CHAPTER 5

[1]Proverbs 7:21-23.

[2]2 Samuel 14:14.

[3]Isaiah 1:18.

[4]Oswald Chambers, *The Place of Help*, quoted in *Rebuilding Your Broken World* by Gordon MacDonald (Nashville: Oliver-Nelson Books, a division of Thomas Nelson, Inc., Publishers, 1988), p. 50.

CHAPTER 6

[1]Proverbs 6:6-8.

[2]Proverbs 22:13.

[3]Proverbs 26:16.

[4]Proverbs 24:30-34.

[5]Deuteronomy 28:12.

[6]Proverbs 13:4.

[7]Quoted in *When I Relax I Feel Guilty* by Tim Hansel (Elgin: David C. Cook, 1981), p. 34.

CHAPTER 7

[1]Proverbs 7:1,5.

[2]Job 31:1.

[3]James 1:14,15 TLB.
[4]2 Samuel 12:13.
[5]2 Samuel 16:22.
[6]1 Corinthians 10:6.
[7]Gordon MacDonald, *Rebuilding Your Broken World* (Nashville: Oliver-Nelson Books, a division of Thomas Nelson, Inc., Publishers, 1988), p. 53.

CHAPTER 8
[1]1 Kings 4:34.
[2]1 Kings 10:1-13.
[3]1 Kings 3:5.
[4]1 Kings 3:12,13.
[5]1 Kings 3:9.
[6]1 Kings 3:24-28.
[7]Proverbs 8:10,11,35.
[8]James 1:5.
[9]Stephen R. Covey, *The Seven Habits of Highly Effective People* (New York: A Fireside Book published by Simon & Schuster, 1989), p. 109.

CHAPTER 9
[1]"Anatomy of a Spiritual Leader," a conversation with Gordon MacDonald in *Leadership,* Fall 1984, Volume V, Number 4, p. 111.
[2]Proverbs 27:17.
[3]Quoted in *The Wit and Wisdom of D. L. Moody* by Stanley and Patricia Gundry, eds. (Grand Rapids: Baker, 1982), pp. 63,64.

CHAPTER 10
[1]Proverbs 10:11.
[2]Proverbs 12:18.
[3]Arthur Gordon, *A Touch of Wonder* (Old Tappan: Fleming H. Revell, 1974), pp. 51,52.
[4]Ugo Bette, "The Burnt Flower Bed," quoted in *No Longer Strangers* by Bruce Larson (Waco: Word Books, Publisher, 1971), p. 56.

CHAPTER 11

[1]*The Desert Christian*, translated by Benedicta Ward, quoted in *Disciplines for the Inner Life* by Bob Benson and Michael W. Benson (Waco: Word Books Publisher, 1985), pp. 251,252.

CHAPTER 12

[1]Dick Gregory, *nigger: AN AUTOBIOGRAPHY,* quoted in *Soundings* by Robert A. Raines (New York: Harper & Row, Publishers, 1970), pp. 94,95.

[2]Bob Benson, *Come Share the Being*, quoted in *Disciplines for the Inner Life* by Bob Benson and Michael W. Benson (Waco: Word Books Publisher, 1985), p. 312.

CHAPTER 13

[1]1 Timothy 6:9.

[2]Luke 12:15.

[3]Proverbs 15:27.

[4]Proverbs 12:11.

[5]Proverbs 14:15.

[6]Proverbs 13:20.

[7]Proverbs 21:5.

[8]Private Journal

CHAPTER 14

[1]Thomas Lickona, "The Return of Character Education," *Educational Leadership*, November 1993, pp. 6,9.

[2]Charles Colson with Nancy R. Pearcey, *A Dance With Deception* (Dallas: Word Publishing, 1993), p. 189.

[3]Ibid., p. 190.

[4]Proverbs 14:34.

[5]Quoted in *America's God and Country Encyclopedia of Quotations* by William J. Federer (Coppel, TX: Fame Publishing, Inc., 1994), pp. 10,11.

[6]Colson and Pearcey, pp. 195,196.

[7]Daniel 9:4,5,17-19.

CHAPTER 15

[1]Proverbs 18:19.

[2]Proverbs 15:32.

[3]Proverbs 10:17.

[4]Ruel Howe, *The Miracle of Dialogue* (Greenwich: The Seabury Press, 1963), p. 93.

CHAPTER 16

[1]C. Roy Angell, *Baskets of Silver* (Nashville: Broadman Press, 1955), pp. 102-104.

[2]Proverbs 16:24.

[3]Taken from *The Daily Study Bible*, "The Letters to the Galatians and Ephesians" by William Barclay (Edinburgh, Scotland: The Saint Andrew Press, 1962), p. 211.

CHAPTER 17

[1]Proverbs 17:17.

[2]John Killinger, *For God's Sake, Be Human* (Waco: Word Books Publisher, 1970), p. 149.

CHAPTER 18

[1]Matthew 27:3-5.

[2]John 8:11.

[3]2 Samuel 24:10,14.

[4]Psalm 9:9.

[5]Psalm 9:10.

[6]Proverbs 18:10.

[7]Hebrews 11:11.

[8]Psalm 145:17.

[9]Deuteronomy 4:31.

[10]Exodus 34:6.

[11]Ephesians 3:20.

[12]Psalm 23:4.

[13]Exodus 3:7.

[14]Exodus 3:8.
[15]Romans 4:21.

CHAPTER 19

[1]Acts 7:22.
[2]Exodus 4:10 TLB.
[3]See Acts 7:23-29.
[4]Proverbs 19:3.
[5]Romans 11:29.
[6]Proverbs 24:16.
[7]Ray A. Kroc, *Grinding It Out* (New York: Berkley, 1978), p. 201.

CHAPTER 20

[1]Paul Tournier, *To Understand Each Other*, translated by John S. Gilmour (Richmond: John Knox Press, 1962), p. 29.
[2]Paul D. Robbins, "Must Men Be Friendless?" *Leadership,* Fall 1984, Volume V, Number 4, p. 25.
[3]*Ibid.*, p. 25.
[4]Proverbs 20:19.
[5]Proverbs 20:5.
[6]Proverbs 12:26.
[7]Tournier, p. 30.

CHAPTER 21

[1]Quoted in *Encyclopedia of 7,700 Illustrations: Signs of the Times* by Paul Lee Tan, Th.D. (Chicago: Assurance Publishers, 1979), p. 618.

CHAPTER 22

[1]Psalm 138:8.
[2]Colossians 3:23.
[3]Matthew 25:21 KJV.
[4]Proverbs 22:29.
[5]Richard Exley, *The Making of a Man* (Tulsa: Honor Books, 1993), p. 186.

CHAPTER 23

[1]Charles Colson with Nancy R. Pearcey, *A Dance With Deception* (Dallas: Word Publishing, 1993), p. 41.
[2]*Ibid.*
[3]Proverbs 29:15.
[4]Richard Exley, *The Making of a Man* (Tulsa: Honor Books, 1993), p. 67.
[5]James Dobson, *Dr. Dobson Answers Your Questions* (Wheaton: Tyndale House Publishers, Inc., 1982), p. 130.

CHAPTER 24

[1]Ilion T. Jones, *God's Everlasting Yes* (Waco: Word Books Publisher, 1969), p. 24.
[2]*Ibid.*
[3]Charles R. Swindoll, *Growing Strong in the Seasons of Life* (Portland: Multnomah Press, 1983), p. 69.
[4]Jones, p. 11.
[5]Proverbs 24:16.
[6]Swindoll, p. 70.

CHAPTER 25

[1]Proverbs 25:20.
[2]John Gray, Ph.D., *Men Are from Mars, Women Are from Venus* (New York: HarperCollins Publishers, Inc., 1992), p. 21.
[3]*Ibid.*, p. 2.

CHAPTER 26

[1]John C. Maxwell, *The Winning Attitude* (Nashville: Thomas Nelson Publishers, 1993), p. 35.
[2]*Ibid.*, p. 32.
[3]Quoted in *Growing Strong in the Seasons of Life* by Charles R. Swindoll (Portland: Multnomah Press, 1983), p. 359.

CHAPTER 27

[1]Quoted in *Familiar Quotations* by John Bartlett, ed. (Boston: Little, Brown and Company, 1955), p. 475.

[2]Charles R. Swindoll, *Growing Strong in the Seasons of Life* (Portland: Multnomah Press, 1983), p. 356.
[3]Proverbs 27:21.
[4]Psalm 75:6,7.
[5]Daniel 6:4.
[6]Daniel 6:5.
[7]Quoted in *Fatal Conceit* by Richard W. Dortch (Green Forest, AR: New Leaf Press, Inc., 1993), p. 57.

CHAPTER 28

[1]Gordon MacDonald, *Rebuilding Your Broken World* (Nashville: Thomas Nelson Publishers, 1988), p. 72.
[2]Psalm 32:3,4.
[3]Psalm 38:4,6-8.
[4]Psalm 32:5.
[5]Psalm 32:1,2.
[6]Proverbs 28:13.
[7]MacDonald, p. 67.

CHAPTER 29

[1]Daniel 1:8.
[2]Sinclair B. Ferguson, *The Communicator's Commentary, Volume 19: Daniel* (Waco: Word, Inc., 1988), pp. 35,36.
[3]*Ibid.*, p. 39.
[4]Proverbs 29:25.
[5]Proverbs 29:25.
[6]Quoted in *Encyclopedia of 7,700 Illustrations: Signs of the Times* by Paul Lee Tan (Chicago: Assurance Publishers, 1979), p. 282.

CHAPTER 30

[1]Isaiah 41:9-13.
[2]Isaiah 41:10-12.
[3]Isaiah 65:24.
[4]Isaiah 41:12,13.

[5]Paul Tournier, *The Meaning of Persons*, quoted in *Reflections on Life's Most Critical Questions* by Paul Tournier (New York: Harper & Row Publishers, 1976), pp. 113,114.

CHAPTER 31

[1]Proverbs 19:14.

[2]Proverbs 31:15,17,18.

[3]Proverbs 31:26.

[4]Proverbs 31:21.

[5]Proverbs 31:25.

[6]Proverbs 31:20.

[7]Proverbs 31:30,31,28.

[8]Proverbs 18:22.

BIBLIOGRAPHY

"Anatomy of a Spiritual Leader," *Leadership,* Fall 1984, Volume V, Number 4.

Angell, C. Roy. *Baskets of Silver.* Nashville: Broadman Press, 1955.

Barclay, William. "The Letters to the Galatians and Ephesians," *The Daily Study Bible.* Edinburgh, Scotland: The Saint Andrew Press, 1962.

Bartlett, John, ed. *Familiar Quotations.* Boston: Little, Brown and Company, 1955.

Benson, Bob, and Benson, Michael W. *Disciplines for the Inner Life.* Waco: Word Books Publisher, 1985.

Colson, Charles with Pearcey, Nancy R. *A Dance With Deception.* Dallas: Word Publishing, 1993.

Covey, Stephen R. *The Seven Habits of Highly Effective People.* New York: A Fireside Book published by Simon & Schuster, 1989.

Dobson, James. *Dr. Dobson Answers Your Questions.* Wheaton: Tyndale House Publishers, Inc., 1982.

Dortch, Richard W. *Fatal Conceit.* Green Forest, AR: New Leaf Press, Inc., 1993.

Exley, Richard. *The Making of a Man.* Tulsa: Honor Books, 1993.

Federer, William J. *America's God and Country Encyclopedia of Quotations.* Coppel, TX: Fame Publishing, Inc., 1994.

Ferguson, Sinclair B. *The Communicator's Commentary, Volume 19: Daniel.* Waco: Word, Inc., 1988.

Gordon, Arthur. *A Touch of Wonder.* Old Tappan: Fleming H. Revell, 1974.

Gray, John. Ph.D., *Men Are from Mars, Women Are from Venus*. New York: Harper Collins Publishers, Inc., 1992.

Gundry, Stanley and Patricia, eds., *The Wit and Wisdom of D. L. Moody*. Grand Rapids: Baker, 1982.

Hansel, Tim. *When I Relax I Feel Guilty*. Elgin: David C. Cook, 1981.

Howe, Ruel. *The Miracle of Dialogue*. Greenwich: The Seabury Press, 1963.

Hubbard, David A. *The Communicator's Commentary Series, Old Testament, Volume 15A: Proverbs*. Dallas: Word Books Publisher, 1989.

Jones, Ilion T. God's *Everlasting Yes*. Waco: Word Books Publisher, 1969.

Killinger, John. *For God's Sake, Be Human*. Waco: Word Books Publisher, 1970.

Kroc, Ray A. *Grinding It Out*. New York: Berkley, 1978.

Larson, Bruce. *No Longer Strangers*. Waco: Word Books Publisher, 1971.

Lickona, Thomas. "The Return of Character Education," *Educational Leadership*, November 1993.

MacDonald, Gordon. *Rebuilding Your Broken World*. Nashville: Oliver-Nelson Books, a division of Thomas Nelson, Inc., Publishers, 1988.

Maxwell, John C. *The Winning Attitude*. Nashville: Thomas Nelson Publishers, 1993.

Quoist, Michel. *Prayers*. Kansas City: Sheed and Ward, 1963.

Raines, Robert A. *Soundings*. New York: Harper & Row, Publishers, 1970.

Robbins, Paul R. "Must Men Be Friendless?" *Leadership,* Fall 1984, Volume V, Number 4.

Swindoll, Charles R. *Growing Strong in the Seasons of Life*. Portland: Multnomah Press, 1983.

Tan, Paul Lee, Th.D. *Encyclopedia of 7,700 Illustrations: Signs of the Times*. Chicago: Assurance Publishers, 1979.

Tournier, Paul. *Reflections on Life's Most Critical Questions*. New York: Harper & Row Publishers, 1976.

Tournier, Paul. *To Understand Each Other*, translated by John S. Gilmour. Richmond: John Knox Press, 1962.

Other books by Richard Exley, available from your local bookstore.

Straight From the Heart for Couples

Straight From the Heart for Dad

Straight From the Heart for Graduates

Straight From the Heart for Mom

Marriage in the Making

The Making of a Man

Abortion

Blue-Collar Christianity

Life's Bottom Line

Perils of Power

The Rhythm of Life

When You Lose Someone You Love

The Other God —Seeing God as He Really Is

The Painted Parable

HB HONOR BOOKS

Tulsa, Oklahoma